NONFICTION READERS

THEA NG

RECENT TITLES IN TEACHER IDEAS PRESS' READERS THEATRE SERIES

Classic Readers Theatre for Young Adults
Suzanne I. Barchers and Jennifer L. Kroll

Science Fiction Readers Theatre
Anthony D. Fredericks

From the Page to the Stage: The Educator's Complete Guide to Readers Theatre
Shirlee Sloyer

Simply Shakespeare: Readers Theatre for Young People
Edited by Jennifer L. Kroll

Character Counts! Promoting Character Education Through Readers Theatre, Grades 2–5
Charla Rene Pfeffinger

Sea Songs: Readers Theatre from the South Pacific
James W. Barnes

Judge for Yourself: Famous American Trials for Readers Theatre
Suzanne I. Barchers

Just Deal with It! Funny Readers Theatre for Life's Not-So-Funny Moments
Diana R. Jenkins

How and Why Stories for Readers Theatre
Judy Wolfman

Born Storytellers: Readers Theatre Celebrates the Lives and Literature of Classic Authors
Ann N. Black

Around the World Through Holidays: Cross Curricular Readers Theatre
Written and Illustrated by Carol Peterson

Wings of Fancy: Using Readers Theatre to Study Fantasy Genre
Joan Garner

NONFICTION READERS THEATRE FOR BEGINNING READERS

Anthony D. Fredericks

Readers Theatre

Teacher Ideas Press

An imprint of Libraries Unlimited
Westport, Connecticut • London

Library of Congress Cataloging-in-Publication Data

Fredericks, Anthony D.
    Nonfiction readers theatre for beginning readers / Anthony D. Fredericks.
        p. cm. — (Readers theatre)
    Includes bibliographical references and index.
    ISBN-13: 978–1–59158–499–5 (alk. paper)
    ISBN-10: 1–59158–499–X (alk. paper)
    1. Children's plays, American. 2. Readers' theater. 3. Drama in education. 4. Activity programs
in education. 5. Science—Study and teaching (Primary) —Activity programs. 6. Communities—
Study and teaching (Primary) — Activity programs. 7. Holidays—Study and teaching (Primary) —
Activity programs. I. Title.
PS625.5.F74 2007
812'.54—dc22   2006037631

British Library Cataloguing in Publication Data is available.

Library of Congress Catalog Card Number: 2006037631
ISBN: 978–1–59158–499–5

First published in 2007

Libraries Unlimited/Teacher Ideas Press, 88 Post Road West, Westport, CT 06881
A Member of the Greenwood Publishing Group, Inc.
www.lu.com

Printed in the United States of America

The paper used in this book complies with the
Permanent Paper Standard issued by the National
Information Standards Organization (Z39.48–1984).

10 9 8 7 6 5 4 3 2 1

To Paula Gilbert—one of the world's great

children's librarians—whose passion for literature is

exceeded only by her effervescent personality, wondrous

repartee, and endearing friendship.

Contents

Part I
Reading Level, First Grade

Part II
Reading Level, Second Grade

Part III
Reading Level, Third Grade

Preface

One of the great pleasures of being a children's author is the opportunity to travel to schools throughout North America and share the joys of writing with kids. Like many visiting writers, I am well prepared to answer the 4 questions most frequently asked of every author:

1. "Where do you get your ideas?"

2. "How much money do you make?"

3. "How old are you?"

4. "Is your wife pretty?"

However, on occasion there is another question that students pose during interactive Q&A sessions. Someone will ask, "Do you always write nonfiction books?" I suspect that that query comes from a steady diet of fictional literature and narrative materials. As a result, some students may have had limited invitations to explore the mysteries and magic of nonfiction. Or, it may be due to a perception that nonfiction is simply the reporting of facts and figures with little or no storytelling involved. Perhaps some students think that nonfiction doesn't have the pizzazz or energy of fictional materials.

However, as an author of more than 3 dozen nature and animal children's books, I have always found nonfiction to be a field that is vibrant, alive, and dynamic. While writing *Under One Rock: Bugs , Slugs, and Other Ughs* (Dawn Publications, 2001), I learned about earthworms in Australia that grow to lengths of 9 feet or so. During the research for *Animal Sharpshooters* (Franklin Watts, 1999), I discovered the bolus spider, which can lasso its enemies with a length of silk. While preparing the manuscript for *Near One Cattail: Turtles, Logs and Leaping Frogs* (Dawn Publications, 2005), I discovered that the Goliath frog is larger than a dinner plate. It's information like this that excites me as a writer (and a "professional student"); it's information like this that helps kids appreciate the wide, wonderful world in which they live.

In a sense, nonfiction literature is a mosaic of our knowledge, a tapestry of our unanswered questions, and a portrait of possibilities. It is not the facts that are important, but rather the concepts that weave those facts together into vibrant understandings and colorful perceptions. Memorizing facts is meaningless and irrelevant; helping students acquire an intellectual framework for dealing with relationships and constructing generalizations is much more important.

This book offers beginning readers a participatory approach to the wide and wonderful world of nonfiction. It is based on the idea that when students are provided with meaningful opportunities to make an "investment of self" in their education, that education will become both relevant and dynamic. *Nonfiction Readers Theatre for Beginning Readers* presents readers theatre scripts that stimulate children to become active participants in selected science and social studies concepts. Students will discover the composition of the earth they live on, they'll take on the roles of dinosaur scientists (paleontologists), and they'll sit beside the pilgrims at the first Thanksgiving. In short, students will assume the personae of scientists, participate in significant historical events, and get a "you are there" perspective that transcends anything they might encounter in a textbook.

Within these pages is a dynamic variety of creative learning possibilities for your classroom. Here, your students will discover an exciting cornucopia of mind-expanding and concept-building experiences—experiences that will reshape their perceptions of what science and social studies are as well as what they can be. In short, readers theatre offers opportunities to make facts come alive. So be prepared for lots of action, lots of drama, and lots of fun!

Let the adventures begin!!

Tony Fredericks

P.S. Oh, by the way, in case you're wondering, my response to question number 4 above is always:

"Of course, she's an enchanted princess!"

Acknowledgments

This book has been endorsed, supported, and nurtured by several people—all of whom deserve a standing ovation and thunderous accolades.

I am particularly indebted to Amanda Jessop, who worked tirelessly to provide the Spanish translations for designated scripts. Her energy and enthusiasm for this project is liberally sprinkled throughout these pages. She truly merits extra recognition and sincere appreciation for her attention to detail, her high level of professionalism, and her ability to work under extremely tight deadlines. Thank you, Amanda!

I am equally appreciative of Dr. Gabriel Abudu, who meticulously checked and verified the accuracy of the translations with his usual brand of dedication and service. His contributions are sincerely appreciated and valued!

I am especially indebted to Suzanne Barchers, who, more than 15 years ago, first introduced me to the overwhelming excitement, unbounded thrills, and unimaginable possibilities of writing readers theatre scripts. She was, and continues to be, an inspiration.

Once again, I applaud (another standing ovation please) the contributions and dedication of my former student, Stephanie Riley, to another literary effort. Steph is in a class by herself—consistently contributing her creative energy and dynamic ideas to every educational venture. She is a teacher of the highest order and I am truly thankful for all her work.

To my long-time friends and colleagues—Paula Gilbert and Judy Wolfman—who were co-partners with me in an extraordinary program of children's books, storytelling, and magical interactions with underserved urban youngsters, I am particularly grateful. Their continuing support and enormous energy are always treasured . . . always celebrated. They truly bring life to literature and literature to life.

And, to all the teachers throughout North America who have used my previous readers theatre books in your classrooms—thank you! The energy you have shared and the stories your students have told are treasured memories of this fantastic literary venture—a journey of wondrous possibilities and a voyage of incredible imagination.

Introduction

Once upon a time, in 1997, I wrote a teacher resource book called *Tadpole Tales and Other Totally Terrific Treats for Readers Theatre* (Teacher Ideas Press)—a book that was specifically designed for teachers in grades 1–3 (all of the scripts were controlled for readability). That book was a collection of "wild and wacky" readers theatre scripts that were adaptations of Mother Goose rhymes and traditional fairy tales. Titles of some of the scripts in that book included:

❖ "The Three Blind Mice Get Smart (Almost)"

❖ "Rub-a-Dub Dub, How Did All Those Guys Get in That Tub?"

❖ "Goldilocks and the Three Hamsters"

❖ "Humpty Dumpty Cracks Up (Film at 11:00)"

❖ "Don't Kiss Sleeping Beauty, She's Got Really Bad Breath"

That book found its way into thousands of primary-level classrooms and library programs around the country. Teachers would use it as a major part of their language arts program. Librarians would buy it and use it to introduce familiar fairy tales as part of their regular library offerings. It soon became a popular and much-loved part of children's initial introductions to literature and learning.

Letters, e-mails, and comments I received from educators across the country attested to the unbelievable joy that came about when readers theatre was made part of classroom and library experiences. Typically, those messages celebrated 3 specific benefits of readers theatre:

1. **Fluency**—"I really like the way readers theatre provides my first grade students with positive models of language use that help build bridges between word recognition and comprehension."

2. **Integrated language arts**—"When children (during library time) participate in readers theatre they can understand and appreciate the interrelationships between reading, writing, listening, and speaking . . . and literature!"

3. **English Language Learners**—"My ELL students benefit from readers theatre because they can see and hear language in action as well as the various ways in which English is used—by me and the other students."

With the success of *Tadpole Tales*, it wasn't too long before teachers and librarians would approach me at conferences and teacher in-service presentations asking for a new volume of readers theatre scripts. They not only requested scripts that could be used with beginning readers, but were equally interested in scripts that focused on nonfiction topics—those typically presented in the science and social studies curricula. Thus was born the idea for this book. But now I think it might be a good idea to take a look at what readers theatre is, its value for beginning readers, and its implications for your classroom or library program.

WHAT IS READERS THEATRE?

Readers theatre is a storytelling device that stimulates the imagination and promotes *all* of the language arts. Simply stated, it is an oral interpretation of a piece of literature read in a dramatic style. Readers theatre is an act of involvement, an opportunity to share, a time to creatively interact with others, and a personal interpretation of what can be or could be. Readers theatre provides numerous opportunities for youngsters to make stories and literature come alive and pulsate with their own unique brand of perception and vision. In so doing, literature becomes personal and reflective —children have a breadth of opportunities to be authentic users of language.

The magic of storytelling has been a tradition of every culture and civilization since the dawn of language. It binds human beings and celebrates their heritage as no other language art can. It is part and parcel of the human experience, because it underscores the values and experiences we cherish as well as those we seek to share with each other. Nowhere is this more important than in today's classroom. Perhaps it is a natural part of who we are—that stories command our attention and help us appreciate the values, ideas, and traditions we hold dear. So, too, should students have those same experiences and those same pleasures.

Storytelling conjures up all sorts of visions and possibilities—faraway lands, magnificent adventures, enchanted princes, beautiful princesses, evil wizards and wicked witches, a few dragons and demons, a couple of castles and cottages, perhaps a mysterious forest or two, and certainly tales of mystery, intrigue, and adventure. These are stories of tradition and timelessness, tales that enchant, mystify, and excite through a marvelous weaving of characters, settings, and plots . . . tales that have stood the test of time. Our senses are stimulated, our mental images are energized, and our experiences are fortified through the magic of storytelling.

Storytelling is also a way of sharing the power and intrigue of nonfiction or expository material. I suppose part of my belief that storytelling is the quintessential classroom activity lies in the fact that it is an opportunity to bring life, vitality, and substance to the two-dimensional letters and words on a printed page. So, too, is it an interpersonal activity—a "never-fail" way to connect with minds and souls and hearts.

When children are provided with regular opportunities to become storytellers, they develop a personal stake in the literature shared. They also begin to cultivate personal interpretations of that literature—interpretations that lead to higher levels of appreciation and comprehension. Practicing and performing stories is an involvement endeavor—one that demonstrates and utilizes numerous languaging activities. So, too, do youngsters learn to listen to their classmates and appreciate a variety of presentations.

READERS THEATRE AND FLUENCY

Of no less importance is the significance of readers theatre as a method to enhance reading fluency. Reading researchers have identified 5 primary areas of reading instruction for all beginning readers: phonemic awareness, phonics, fluency, vocabulary, and comprehension. When teachers and librarians incorporate readers theatre into their respective programs, youngsters are offered multiple opportunities to, as one first-grade teacher put it, "understand the rhythm and flow of language."

Fluency is the ability to read text accurately and quickly. It's reading in which words are recognized automatically. When fluent readers read, they group words quickly to help them gain meaning from what they read. Their oral reading sounds natural and their silent reading is smooth and unencumbered by an overemphasis on word-by-word analysis. Fluent readers are those who do not need to concentrate on the decoding of words; rather, they can direct their attention to their comprehension of text. In short, fluent readers are able to recognize words and comprehend them at the same time. They are able to make connections between their background knowledge and ideas in a book or other piece of writing. I often like to think of fluency as the essential stepping stone between phonetic ability and comprehension.

It's important to remember that fluency is something that develops over time. Fluency instruction must be integrated into all aspects of the reading program as the "bridge" that students need to be successful comprehenders. Fluency is not an isolated element of the reading curriculum—rather, it is an essential component that models and provides active involvement opportunities for students as they transition from decoding to comprehension. A study by the National Assessment of Educational Progress (NAEP, 2001) found a direct correlation between fluency and reading comprehension. In fact, students who score low on measures of fluency also score low on measures of comprehension. The implication was that efforts designed to foster fluency development will have a direct impact on students' growth and development in comprehension.

Not surprising, one of the most effective ways teachers can promote fluency development—particularly for beginning readers—is through the use of readers theatre. Its advantages are twofold: (1) it offers positive models of fluent reading as demonstrated by a teacher or other accomplished readers, and (2) it provides beginning readers with a legitimate reason for rereading text in an enjoyable and engaging format. Students get to practice fluency in authentic texts and in authentic situations. Reading is portrayed as a pleasurable activity—it has both purpose and interest. As students take on the roles of characters, they also take on the roles of competent readers.

WHAT IS THE VALUE OF READERS THEATRE?

I like to think of readers theatre as a way to interpret nonfiction information without the constraints of skills, rote memorization, or assignments. Readers theatre allows children to breathe life and substance into factual data—an interpretation that is colored by kids' unique perspectives, experiences, and vision. It is, in fact, the readers' interpretation of an event that is intrinsically more valuable than some predetermined and/or preordained "translation" (something that might be found in a teacher's manual or curriculum guide, for example).

With that in mind, I'd like to share with you some of the many values I see in readers theatre:

❖ Readers theatre is a participatory event. The characters as well as the audience are intimately involved in the design, structure, and delivery of the story. As such, children begin to realize that learning science or social studies is not a solitary activity, but one that can be shared and discussed with others.

❖ Readers theatre stimulates curiosity and enthusiasm for learning. It allows children to experience learning in a supportive and nonthreatening format that underscores their active involvement.

❖ Since it is the performance that drives readers theatre, children are given more opportunities to invest themselves and their personalities in the production of a readers theatre. The same story may be subject to several different presentations depending on the group or the individual youngsters involved. As such, children learn that readers theatre can be explored in a host of ways and a host of possibilities.

❖ Children are given numerous opportunities to learn about the major features of selected science or social studies concepts.

❖ Readers theatre is informal and relaxed. It does not require elaborate props, scenery, or costumes. It can be set up in any classroom or library. It does not require large sums of money to "make it happen." And, it can be "put on" in any kind of environment—formal or informal.

❖ Readers theatre stimulates the imagination and the creation of visual images. It has been substantiated that when youngsters are provided with opportunities to create their own mental images, their comprehension and appreciation of a piece of writing will be enhanced considerably. Since only a modicum of formal props and "set up" are required for any readers theatre production, the participants and audience are encouraged to create supplemental "props" in their minds—props that may be more elaborate and exquisite than those found in the most lavish of plays.

❖ Readers theatre enhances the development of cooperative learning strategies. It requires youngsters to work together toward a common goal and supports their efforts in doing so. Readers theatre is not a competitive activity, but rather a cooperative one in which children share, discuss, and band together for the good of the production.

❖ Teachers and librarians have also discovered that readers theatre is an excellent way in which to enhance the development of communication skills. Voice projection, intonation, inflection, and pronunciation skills are all promoted within and throughout any readers theatre production.

❖ The development and enhancement of self-concept is facilitated through readers theatre. Since children are working in concert with other children in a supportive atmosphere, their self-esteem mushrooms accordingly. Again, the emphasis is on the presentation, not necessarily the performers. As such, youngsters have opportunities to develop levels of self-confidence and self-assurance that would not normally be available in more traditional class productions.

❖ Creative and critical thinking are enhanced through the utilization of readers theatre. Children are active participants in the interpretation and delivery of a story; as such, they develop thinking skills that are divergent rather than convergent, and interpretive skills that are supported rather than directed.

❖ Readers theatre is fun! Children of all ages have delighted in using readers theatre for many years. It is delightful and stimulating, encouraging and fascinating, relevant and personal. Indeed, try as I might, I have not been able to locate a single instance (or group of children) in which (or for whom) readers theatre would not be an appropriate learning activity. It is a strategy filled with a cornucopia of possibilities and promises.

Readers theatre holds the promise of "energizing" your classroom language arts curriculum, stimulating your library program, and fostering an active and deeper engagement of students in all the dynamics of books, literature, and reading. For both classroom teachers and school librarians its benefits are enormous and its implications endless.

Presentation Suggestions

It is important to remember that there is no single way to present readers theatre. What follows are some ideas you and the youngsters with whom you work may wish to keep in mind as you put on the productions in this book—whether in a classroom setting or the school library.

PREPARING SCRIPTS

One of the advantages of using readers theatre in the classroom is the lack of extra work or preparation time necessary to get "up and running." By using the scripts in this book, your preparation time is minimal.

❖ After a script has been selected for presentation, make sufficient copies. A copy of the script should be provided for each actor. In addition, making 2 or 3 extra copies (1 for you and "replacement" copies for scripts that are accidentally damaged or lost) is also a good idea. Copies for the audience are unnecessary and are not suggested.

❖ Each script can be bound between 2 sheets of colored construction paper or poster board. Bound scripts tend to formalize the presentation a little and lend an air of professionalism to the actors.

❖ Highlight each character's speaking parts with different color highlighter pens. This helps youngsters track their parts without being distracted by the dialogue of others.

❖ After duplicating the necessary number of English/Spanish scripts (according to the designated number of characters), use a highlighter pen to highlight all of the English lines or all of the Spanish lines (as applicable) in each copy of the script. Then instruct the students to focus solely on the blue lines (or green lines, or pink lines, etc.) in their reading of the script. This will help keep them focused on just the English lines or Spanish lines (as appropriate).

STARTING OUT

Introducing the concept of readers theatre to your students for the first time may be as simple as sharing a script with the entire class and "walking" youngsters through the design and delivery of that script.

❖ Emphasize that a readers theatre performance does not require any memorization of the script. It's the interpretation and performance that count.

❖ You may wish to read through an entire script aloud, taking on the various roles. Let students know how easy and comfortable this process is.

❖ Encourage selected volunteers to read assigned parts of a sample script to the entire class. Readers should stand or sit in a circle so that other classmates can observe them.

❖ Provide opportunities for additional rereadings using other volunteers. Plan time to discuss the ease of presentation and the different interpretations offered by different readers.

- ❖ Readers should have an opportunity to practice their script before presenting it to an audience. Take some time to discuss voice intonation, facial gestures, body movements, and other features that could be used to enhance the presentation.

- ❖ Allow children the opportunity to suggest their own modifications, adaptations, or interpretations of the script. They will undoubtedly be "in tune" with the interests and perceptions of their peers and can offer some distinctive and personal interpretations.

- ❖ Encourage students to select nonstereotypical roles within any readers theatre script. For example, boys can take on female roles and girls can take on male roles, the smallest person in the class can take on the role of a giant dinosaur, or a shy student can take on the role of a boastful, bragging historical figure. Provide sufficient opportunities for students to expand and extend their appreciation of readers theatre through a variety of "out of character" roles.

STAGING

Staging involves the physical location of the readers as well as any necessary movements. Unlike a more formal play, the movements are often minimal. The emphasis is more on presentation and less on action.

- ❖ For most presentations, readers will stand and/or sit on stools or chairs. The physical location of each reader has been indicated for each of the scripts in this book.

- ❖ If there are many characters in the presentation, it may be advantageous to have characters in the rear (upstage) standing while those in the front (downstage) are placed on stools or chairs. This ensures that the audience will both see and hear each actor.

- ❖ Usually all of the characters will be on stage throughout the duration of the presentation. For most presentations it is not necessary to have characters enter and exit. If you place the characters on stools, they can face the audience when they are involved in a particular scene and then turn around whenever they are not involved in a scene.

- ❖ You may wish to make simple hand-lettered signs with the name of each character. Loop a piece of string or yarn through each sign and hang it around the neck of each respective character. That way, the audience will know the identity of each character throughout the presentation.

- ❖ Each reader will have her or his own copy of the script in a paper cover (see above). If possible, use a music stand for each reader's script (this allows readers to use their hands for dramatic interpretations as necessary).

- ❖ Several presentations have a narrator to set up the story. The narrator serves to establish the place and time of the story for the audience so that the characters can "jump into" their parts from the beginning of the story. Typically, the narrator is separated from the other "actors" and can be identified by a simple sign.

PROPS

Two of the positive features of readers theatre are its ease of preparation and its ease of presentation. Informality is a hallmark of any readers theatre script.

- ❖ Much of the setting for a story should take place in the audience's mind. Elaborate scenery is not necessary—simple props are often the best. For example:
  - A branch or potted plant can serve as a tree.
  - A drawing on the chalkboard can illustrate a building.
  - A hand-lettered sign can designate one part of the staging area as a particular scene (e.g., swamp, castle, field, forest).
  - Children's toys can be used for uncomplicated props (e.g., telephone, vehicles).
  - A sheet of aluminum foil or a remnant of blue cloth can be used to simulate a lake or pond.

- ❖ Costumes for the actors are unnecessary. A few simple items may be suggested by students. For example:
  - Hats, scarves, or aprons can be used by major characters.
  - A paper cutout can serve as a tie, button, or badge.
  - Old clothing (borrowed from parents) can be used as warranted.

- ❖ Some teachers and librarians have discovered that the addition of appropriate background music or sound effects can enhance a readers theatre presentation.

- ❖ It's important to remember that the emphasis in readers theatre is on the reading—not on any accompanying "features." The best presentations are often the simplest.

DELIVERY

I've often found it advantageous to let students know that the only difference between a readers theatre presentation and a movie role is the fact that they will have a script in their hands. This allows them to focus more on presenting rather than memorizing a script.

- ❖ When first introduced to readers theatre, students often have a tendency to "read into" their scripts. Encourage students to look up from their scripts and interact with other characters or the audience as necessary

- ❖ Practicing the script beforehand can eliminate the problem of students burying their heads in the pages. In so doing, children understand the need to involve the audience as much as possible in the development of the story.

- ❖ Voice projection and delivery are important in allowing the audience to understand character actions. The proper mood and intent need to be established—aspects that are possible when children are familiar and comfortable with each character's "style."

- ❖ Again, the emphasis is on delivery, so be sure to suggest different types of voice (i.e., angry, irritated, calm, frustrated, excited, etc.) that children may wish to use for their particular character(s).

ENGLISH LANGUAGE LEARNERS (ELL)

Children who are learning English as a second language face numerous challenges—challenges that native speakers seldom encounter. For example, students whose native language is Spanish pronounce selected letters (especially vowels) quite differently than English-speaking children. In

Spanish, all the consonants (with the exception of *h*) are sounded, whereas in English there are several silent consonants (e.g., *k* as in knot, *g* as in gnu, *w* as in write).

Readers theatre offers ELL students a practical model of language use—one that can help them make the transition from their native language to English. Here are a few points to consider:

❖ For selected scripts in this book, there are Spanish versions. Invite your ELL students to present the Spanish version of a script immediately after an "English presentation."

❖ Invite ELL students to "teach" a Spanish version of a script to non-Spanish-speaking students.

❖ Use the Spanish scripts as read-aloud opportunities for all students. After reading a Spanish script, read its English equivalent to students.

❖ Tape record selected scripts (in English) and invite ELL students to follow along with a printed version.

❖ Use words from the English scripts along with their equivalents from the Spanish scripts to construct bilingual flash cards and word walls for children.

POST-PRESENTATION

As a wise author once said, "The play's the thing." So it is with readers theatre. In other words, the mere act of presenting a readers theatre script is complete in and of itself. It is not necessary, or even required, to do any type of formalized evaluation after readers theatre. Once again, the emphasis is on informality. Readers theatre should and can be a pleasurable and stimulating experience for children.

What follows are a few ideas you may want to share with students. In doing so, you will be providing youngsters with important learning opportunities that extend and promote all aspects of your language arts, science, or social studies program.

❖ After a presentation, discuss with students how the script enhanced or altered the original story.

❖ Invite students to suggest other characters who could be added to the script.

❖ Invite students to suggest new or alternate dialogue for various characters

❖ Invite students to suggest new or different setting(s) for the script.

❖ Invite students to talk about their reactions to various characters' expressions, tone of voice, presentations, or dialogues.

❖ After a presentation, invite youngsters to suggest any modifications or changes needed in the script.

Presenting a readers theatre script need not be an elaborate or extensive production. As children become more familiar with and polished in using readers theatre, they will be able to suggest a multitude of presentation possibilities for future scripts. It is important to help children assume a measure of self-initiated responsibility in the delivery of any readers theatre. In so doing, you will be helping to ensure their personal engagement and active participation in this most valuable of language arts activities.

Bonus Features

This resource has been especially designed for classroom teachers, school librarians, or reading specialists who work with beginning readers; specifically youngsters in grades 1–3. Teaching children in these grades has always been a challenge, yet the opportunities for literacy growth and development are enormous. Readers theatre has proven itself as one way you can help children learn language in context in addition to enhancing your overall reading or language arts program.

To help make your task of teaching primary-level youngsters a little easier, several bonus features have been included throughout the book. Please consider these as important elements in the introduction and use of readers theatre in your classroom or library.

1. **Readability**—Each of the scripts in this book has been assessed according to its readability—or its appropriateness for a specific reading grade level. You will discover 10 scripts written at the first-grade reading level, 8 scripts at the second-grade level, and 8 scripts at the third-grade level. The primary factors in determining the readability of a script were sentence length and average number of syllables per word. With this in mind, you will be able to use scripts that are appropriate for the reading level of an entire class or for selected individuals within a class. You should feel free to use scripts from any or all levels.

2. **Content standards**—The scripts in this book have all been developed based on common content standards for grades 1–3 for both science and social studies. These content standards have been gleaned from those promulgated by the National Science Teachers Association (NSTA) and the National Council on the Social Studies (NCSS). Specific standards for grades 1–3 include the following:

Science

- Properties of objects and materials
- Position and motion of objects
- Light, heat, electricity, and magnetism
- Characteristics of organisms
- Life cycles of organisms
- Organisms and environment
- Properties of earth materials
- Objects in the sky
- Changes in earth and sky
- Science and technology
- Personal health

Social studies

- Culture
- Time, continuity, and change
- People, places, and environment
- Individual development and identity

- Individuals, groups, and institutions
- Power, authority, and governance
- Production, distribution, and consumption
- Science, technology, and society
- Global connections
- Civic ideals and practices

You will discover that the use of these readers theatre scripts will assist you in promoting and adhering to basic science and social studies standards. This provides you with wonderful learning opportunities that effectively integrate the language arts curriculum with the science or social studies curriculum. The result can be an exciting and dynamic learning experience for all students.

3. **Scripts in Spanish**—In each of the three parts of this book there are three Spanish scripts, each integrated into the corresponding English script (total, 9 scripts). You are encouraged to use these scripts with both your ELL students and your English-speaking students. In addition to the suggestions offered above (in the "English Language Learners (ELL)" section), here are some additional ideas you may wish to consider regarding these specific scripts:

- Use selected words from the Spanish scripts as "sight words" for your English-speaking students. Post these on an appropriate bulletin board.

- Provide students with "mini-lessons" in Spanish to help them learn the language of the ELL students in the class.

- Invite English-speaking students to present an "English" script to be followed by the "Spanish" equivalent immediately thereafter.

- Reverse the sequence of presentation as described above.

- Invite both English-speaking and ELL students to present an English script. Follow up by asking selected parent volunteers to present the Spanish equivalent to the class.

- Reverse the sequence above by asking parent volunteers to present an English script with a student follow-up of the Spanish script.

- Invite parent volunteers to make audiorecordings of both the English and Spanish scripts. Provide opportunities for students to listen to these recordings.

- Pair up English-speaking students with ELL "buddies" for informal tutoring sessions using the scripts in this book.

4. **Experiments and activities**—For each script there is one experiment (science) or 1 to 2 hands-on activities (social studies) you can share with your students. These are offered to help you extend the learning opportunities for your students. They provide real-world learning opportunities that assist students in integrating the concept(s) promoted in a script with the world outside the classroom or library. Here a few suggested uses of these experiments and activities:

- Invite students to participate in an experiment or activity prior to presenting an accompanying readers theatre script.

- Invite students to participate in an experiment or activity after presenting an accompanying readers theatre script.

- After reading aloud a selected nonfiction trade book (on a specific topic), follow up with an experiment or activity and then a readers theatre script.

- After reading aloud a selected nonfiction trade book (on a specific topic), follow up with a readers theatre script and then an experiment or activity.

- Present students with an experiment or activity, then perform a readers theatre script, and finally read aloud a selected nonfiction trade book (on a relevant topic).

- Present students with an experiment or activity, then read aloud a selected nonfiction trade book (on a relevant topic), and finally invite them to perform the appropriate readers theatre script.

- Invite students to present a selected readers theatre script, then read aloud a selected nonfiction trade book (on a relevant topic), and finally do an accompanying experiment or activity.

- Invite students to present a selected readers theatre script, then do an accompanying experiment or activity, and finally read aloud an appropriate nonfiction trade book.

5. **Selected nonfiction literature**—Listed with each readers theatre script is a selection of specific nonfiction titles. Each of the books supports the content standards promulgated through the script. In addition, each book offers additional factual information in support of those standards. You are encouraged to provide students with these books as they are available in your classroom or school library. In addition, you will discover several opportunities to combine the information in these books with that in a specific script (see suggestions in item 4 above). You may also wish to develop selected books into appropriate readers theatre scripts for use by your students.

These are not meant to be exhaustive lists, but rather suggestions that can assist you in providing students with a well-rounded exposure to the wide and wonderful world of nonfiction. As new books are published and reviewed each year, you are encouraged to add additional titles to these listings.

References

Fredericks, Anthony D. 1993. *Frantic Frogs and Other Frankly Fractured Folktales for Readers Theatre*. Westport, CT: Teacher Ideas Press.

———. 1997. *Tadpole Tales and Other Totally Terrific Treats for Readers Theatre*. Westport, CT: Teacher Ideas Press.

———. 2000. *Silly Salamanders and Other Slightly Stupid Stories for Readers Theatre*. Westport, CT: Teacher Ideas Press.

———. 2001. *Readers Theatre for American History*. Westport, CT: Teacher Ideas Press.

———. 2002. *Science Fiction Readers Theatre*. Westport, CT: Teacher Ideas Press.

———. 2007. *Mother Goose Readers Theatre for Beginning Readers*. Westport, CT: Teacher Ideas Press.

Part I

Reading Level, First Grade

Flowers and Plants

(Learning about Plants)

DISCIPLINE

Life science

SCIENCE CONTENT STANDARD

Characteristics of organisms

SUMMARY

This script introduces students to the 3 critical features of any plant: leaves, roots, and stem. While some students may be familiar with these plant features, this presentation underscores the fact that these parts are present in almost any plant.

PROPS

Two different plants will be necessary for this script. One should be a flowering plant (gently removed from a pot). The other should be any other type of plant (perhaps a vegetable, e.g., bean plant, corn plants) gently removed from a garden.

PRESENTATION SUGGESTIONS

Students should be standing throughout this presentation. They should be speaking to each other throughout, but in voices that are loud enough for members of the audience to hear. You may wish to quickly introduce the 3 plant parts to the players before they present the script.

EXPERIMENT/ACTIVITY

Here is an experiment you may wish to share with students upon completion of the script.

Materials

1 fresh stalk of celery

2 glasses of water

red and blue food coloring

dinner knife

Procedure

Put the 2 glasses of water side by side. Place 4 drops of red food coloring in one glass and 4 drops of blue food coloring in the other glass. Cut off the dried, bottom end of the celery stalk and then cut the stalk up the middle from the bottom of the stalk to about three-quarters up the stalk. Stand one-half of the celery stalk in the red water and the other half of the stalk in the blue water. For the next several hours check on the celery stalk.

Results

The blue water will move up the part of the celery stalk placed in the blue water. The red water will move up the part of the celery stalk placed in the red water.

Explanation

All plants have special tubes in their stems. These tubes are like drinking straws and move water from the roots up through the stems and into the leaves. This allows a plant to get the water and food needed for it to grow and develop. The red and blue colored water moves up the stem (stalk) of the celery just like it does in any other plant. Roots take in the water from the soil and the stem transports the water from the roots up to the leaves (using a process known as osmosis).

SUGGESTED LITERATURE

Batten, Mary. *Hungry Plants*. New York: Bantam Doubleday Dell Books for Young Readers, 2004.

Branigan, Carrie, and Richard Dunne. *All Kinds of Plants*. Mankato, MN: Smart Apple Media, 2005.

Fowler, Allan. *From Seed to Plant*. New York: Scholastic, 2001.

Spilsbury, Louise, and Richard Spilsbury. *What Is a Plant?* Portsmouth, NH: Heinemann Library, 2005.

Flowers and Plants

(Learning about Plants)

Las flores y las plantas (Aprender sobre las plantas)

STAGING: The narrator stands to the side of the other characters. The three characters may stand and move around or may be seated on stools or chairs. Student 2 will need a flower, such as a daisy or dandelion. The flower should be removed from a pot or the ground (the roots need to be exposed). Student 3 should have another type of plant such as a bean plant or weed (also with the roots exposed).

```
Student 1
   X
              Student 2                    Narrator
                 X                            X
Student 3
   X
```

NARRATOR: Plants grow. Some plants are tall. Trees are tall. Some plants grow in water. Seaweed is a water plant. Flowers are plants, too. Let's look at a flower.

EL NARRADOR(A): Las plantas crecen. Algunas plantas son altas. Los árboles son altos. Algunas plantas crecen en el agua. El alga es una planta del agua. Las flores son plantas, también. Miremos a una flor.

STUDENT 1: What do you have in your hand?

ESTUDIANTE 1: ¿Qué tienes en la mano?

STUDENT 2: This is a plant.

ESTUDIANTE 2: Esta es una planta.

STUDENT 1: How do you know it's a plant?

ESTUDIANTE 1: ¿Cómo sabes que es una planta?

STUDENT 2: Because it has some special parts.

ESTUDIANTE 2: Porque tiene algunas partes especiales.

STUDENT 1: Like what?

ESTUDIANTE 1: ¿Cómo qué?

STUDENT 2: A plant has leaves [points].

ESTUDIANTE 2: Una planta tiene hojas [señalando].

STUDENT 3: And, a plant has roots [points].

ESTUDIANTE 3: Y, una planta tiene raíces [señalando].

STUDENT 1: What is that long thing [points to stem]?

ESTUDIANTE 1: ¿Qué es esa cosa larga [señalando al tallo]?

STUDENT 2: That is called a stem.

ESTUDIANTE 2: Esa se llama un tallo.

STUDENT 3: The plant stem can be soft.

ESTUDIANTE 3: El tallo de una planta puede ser blando.

STUDENT 2: Or, sometimes it is hard.

ESTUDIANTE 2: O, a veces es duro.

STUDENT 1: What does it do?

ESTUDIANTE 1: ¿Qué hace?

STUDENT 3: It holds up the flower.

ESTUDIANTE 3: Sostiene la flor.

STUDENT 2: And water goes up the stem.

ESTUDIANTE 2: Y el agua sube el tallo.

STUDENT 1: Where does it go?

ESTUDIANTE 1: ¿Adónde va?

STUDENT 3: It goes from the roots to the flower.

ESTUDIANTE 3: Va de las raíces a la flor.

STUDENT 3: So, a plant has three parts. It has leaves. It has roots. It has a stem.

ESTUDIANTE 3: Entonces, una planta tiene tres partes. Tiene hojas. Tiene raíces. Tiene un tallo.

STUDENT 1: Is a flower a plant?

ESTUDIANTE 1: ¿Es una flor una planta?

STUDENT 2: Sure. Look. This flower has leaves [points]. This flower has roots [points]. And, this flower has a stem [points].

ESTUDIANTE 2: Claro. Mira. Esta flor tiene hojas [señalando]. Esta flor tiene raíces [señalando]. Y, esta flor tiene un tallo [señalando].

STUDENT 1: So, a flower is a plant?

ESTUDIANTE 1: Entonces, ¿es una flor un tipo de planta?

STUDENT 3: Right.

ESTUDIANTE 3: Correcto.

STUDENT 1: So, are all plants the same?

ESTUDIANTE 1: Entonces, ¿son todas plantas las mismas?

STUDENT 2: No, plants can be different.

ESTUDIANTE 2: No, las plantas pueden ser diferentes.

STUDENT 3: Plants can be the same . . . .

ESTUDIANTE 3: Las plantas pueden ser las mismas . . . .

STUDENT 2: . . . or different.

ESTUDIANTE 2: . . . o diferentes.

STUDENT 3: Plants can have different shapes.

ESTUDIANTE 3: Las plantas pueden tener formas diferentes.

STUDENT 2: Like round. Or tall. Or short. Or flat.

ESTUDIANTE 2: Como redondas. O altas. O bajas. O planas.

STUDENT 3: Plants can have different colors.

ESTUDIANTE 3: Las plantas pueden tener colores diferentes.

STUDENT 1: I know, I know! Like red. Or green. Or yellow. Or blue.

ESTUDIANTE 1: ¡Ya sé, ya sé! Como rojo. O verde. O amarillo. O azul.

STUDENT 2: Like all the colors of the rainbow.

ESTUDIANTE 2: Como todos los colores del arco iris.

NARRATOR: Flowers are plants. A daisy is a plant. A rose is a plant. A lily is a plant. Look around. What flowers do you know?

EL NARRADOR(A): Las flores son plantas. Una margarita es una planta. Una rosa es una planta. Un lirio es una planta. Echa una mirada. ¿Qué flores conoces?

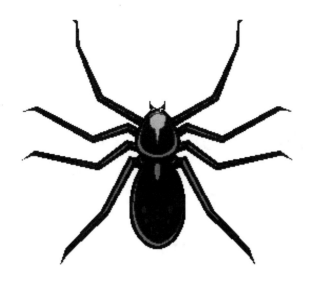

Creepy, Crawly Things

(Learning about Animals)

DISCIPLINE

Life science

SCIENCE CONTENT STANDARD

Characteristics of organisms

SUMMARY

Youngsters are always amazed at the incredible variety of animal species in the world. Interestingly, scientists aren't even sure of the exact number of species because many are becoming extinct even before they are discovered (particularly in the Amazon rain forest). The study of animals continues to be one of the most exciting areas of discovery for any elementary classroom.

PROPS

No props are necessary for this presentation.

PRESENTATION SUGGESTIONS

You may wish to have selected photos of various types of animals posted on the wall behind the characters in this script. Although they aren't necessary, you may wish to display photos of the specific creatures mentioned in the script.

EXPERIMENT/ACTIVITY

Here's a simple activity you can share with your students throughout the school year. I used to do this activity with kindergarten kids, and we called it "Backyard Research."

Materials

4 sharpened pencils

string

magnifying glasses

Procedure

Invite the students to go outside and select a grassy area (part of a yard, lawn, or playground). You may wish to check first to be sure that the area selected is not dried out and/or that it will have sufficient "inhabitants." Encourage them to push 4 sharpened pencils into the soil in a 1-foot-square pattern. Invite students to tie string around the tops of the pencils, making a miniature "boxing ring" on the ground.

Invite youngsters to get down on their hands and knees and look closely inside the "square." Encourage them to make any necessary notes about the different types of animals they see inside the ring. They should note the movements, habits, or behaviors of any animals (ants, grasshoppers, caterpillars, worms) as they travel (jump, crawl, slither) through the ring. Encourage youngsters to visit their "rings" frequently over a period of several weeks. You may wish to inform students that they may not see things immediately and that they may need to observe over a period of time. For young students, you may want to limit their observation time in accordance with their level of patience.

Results

Students will discover a wide variety of critters.

Explanation

Many animals, especially the smallest members of the animal kingdom, are often taken for granted. This activity provides students with an opportunity to become more aware of the wide variety of creatures in a very small arena. They will be amazed to discover the seemingly infinite array of species. This can then serve as a platform for discussion about the almost limitless variety of animals that are alive throughout the world today. Students may wish to follow up with some research on the organisms they have observed. and to perhaps do a little research to identify what they have seen.

SUGGESTED LITERATURE

Murawski, Darlyne A. *Animal Faces*. New York: Sterling Publishing, 2005.

Taylor, Barbara. *Insects*. New York: Kingfisher, 2006.

Wallace, Karen. *A Trip to the Zoo*. New York: DK Publishing, 2003.

Wallace, Karen. *Wild Baby Animals*. New York: DK Publishing, 2000.

Woelfle, Gretchen. *Animal Families, Animal Friends*. Chanhassen, MN: Northwood Press, 2005.

Creepy, Crawly Things

(Learning about Animals)

STAGING: This script has 5 speaking parts and no narrator. The characters can stand around in a loose formation as though they are talking things over on the playground.

```
Charlie
   X          Bruce
                X          Taylor
                             X
              Hernando
                 X          Rocky
                              X
```

CHARLIE: Hey, guess what?

BRUCE: What?

CHARLIE: Did you know how many animals there are?

TAYLOR: A hundred?

CHARLIE: No.

HERNANDO: A thousand?

CHARLIE: No.

ROCKY: A million!

CHARLIE: No, again. There are millions and millions of different animals all over the world.

BRUCE: Wow, I didn't know that!

CHARLIE: Yes, and they are all different.

TAYLOR: Yes, he's right. They are different in many ways.

HERNANDO: There are some animals that are big.

ROCKY: Like a whale or an elephant.

CHARLIE: And there are some animals that are small.

BRUCE: Like a flea or a fly.

TAYLOR: Yes. And some animals have fur.

HERNANDO: Like a bear or a mouse.

ROCKY: And, some animals have feathers.

CHARLIE: Like a turkey or a robin.

BRUCE: And some animals have shells.

TAYLOR: Like a turtle or a clam.

HERNANDO: Some animals have four legs.

ROCKY: Like a giraffe or a cat.

CHARLIE: And some animals have two legs.

BRUCE: Like a gorilla or a chicken.

TAYLOR: And, there are some animals that have no legs.

HERNANDO: Like a snake or a worm.

ROCKY: Some animals live on land.

CHARLIE: Like a snail or a buffalo.

BRUCE: And some animals live in the water.

TAYLOR: Like a dolphin or a shark.

HERNANDO: And some animals live in the sky.

ROCKY: Like an eagle or a butterfly.

CHARLIE: Some animals eat plants.

BRUCE: Like a caterpillar or a deer.

TAYLOR: And some animals eat other animals.

HERNANDO: Like a tiger or a lizard.

ROCKY: Wow, there are a lot of different animals.

CHARLIE: But, don't forget. All animals need three things.

BRUCE: What's that?

TAYLOR: They all need food.

HERNANDO: And they all need water.

ROCKY: And they all need air to breathe.

CHARLIE: So, lots of animals. And, lots of animals to learn about.

ALL: We can't wait!

From *Nonfiction Readers Theatre for Beginning Readers* by Anthony D. Fredericks. Westport, CT: Teacher Ideas Press.

It's Alive

(Living and Nonliving Things)

DISCIPLINE

Life science

SCIENCE CONTENT STANDARD

Characteristics of organisms

SUMMARY

Students are introduced to 3 of the elements of living things. Children often take living and nonliving things for granted. This script, however, helps them begin thinking about the significant differences between these 2 classes of items in the natural world.

PROPS

Place the following items on the table in the middle of the staging area: a rock, a toy car, a large photo of an elephant, and a flowering plant. You may wish to adjust the specific items according to their availability (if so, please modify the script as necessary).

PRESENTATION SUGGESTIONS

The 4 major players will be seated around the table. The narrator has a single speaking part and can exit after her or his line is spoken.

EXPERIMENT/ACTIVITY

Here's a simple activity students can use over an extended period of time (2 to 3 weeks).

Materials

large sheet of newsprint

markers

old magazines

safety scissors

appropriate adhesive

Procedure

Tape a large sheet of newsprint on one wall of the classroom. Divide the sheet into 3 columns using one of the markers. At the top of the first column print the word "Growing." At the top of the second column print the words "Needs Water." At the top of the third column print the words "Has Parents."

Provide students with several old magazine and safety scissors. Invite them to look through the magazine for examples of plants or animals that could be cut out and placed in one of the columns on the chart. As each picture is selected and cut out, invite students to bring the photos to you to be pasted onto the chart. (Each student may wish to indicate a photo's appropriate placement on the chart.)

Results

The chart will record the characteristics of living things and several representative examples.

Explanation

As described in this script, living things have several distinguishing characteristics, including the ability to grow, the need for water, and parents. Students will be able to see these features indicated on a large wall chart.

SUGGESTED LITERATURE

Fredericks, Anthony D. *Under One Rock: Bugs, Slugs, and Other Ughs.* Nevada City, CA: Dawn Publications, 2001.

Zoehfeld, Kathleen Weidner. *What's Alive?* New York: HarperCollins, 1995.

It's Alive

(Living and Nonliving Things)

STAGING: The narrator stands in the front and to the side of the staging area. The other characters are seated around a table on which several items have been placed. As each character speaks she or he will pick up a designated object and hold it so that the audience can clearly see it.

```
                        Bob              Sarah
                         X                 X
                              (table)
                       Clifton            Kasha
                         X                 X
        Narrator
           X
```

NARRATOR: Good morning. Welcome to our science class. We have a puzzle. Let's see if it can be solved.

BOB: [holds rock] What is this thing?

CLIFTON: It's a rock.

BOB: How do you know?

CLIFTON: Because it's not alive.

BOB: Not alive. What do you mean?

KASHA: I know. It's not alive because it can't grow.

SARAH: That's right. All living things grow.

BOB: Are trees living things?

CLIFTON: Yes. Trees are living because they grow.

BOB: What else?

KASHA: [holds a plant] This plant is a living thing.

BOB: Why?

SARAH: It's a living thing because it grows. It's also a living thing because it needs water and air to grow.

BOB: So, if something needs water to grow, then it must be a living thing.

KASHA: That's right, Bob.

BOB: [holds photo of elephant] Let's see. This elephant can grow.

CLIFTON: That's right.

BOB: And, this elephant needs water.

SARAH: That's right.

BOB: So, that means that this elephant is a living thing.

ALL: THAT'S RIGHT!

BOB: What else do I need to know?

KASHA: Well, living things have parents.

BOB: Do all living things have parents?

CLIFTON: Yes they do. Elephant babies have parents. Plants make seeds. The seeds grow into new plants. And, children have parents.

BOB: So, that means that all of us [points] are living things?

ALL: THAT'S RIGHT!

BOB: O.K. let's see what how this works. (holds up toy car) This is not a living thing because it doesn't grow.

SARAH: And it doesn't need water.

KASHA: And it doesn't have parents.

BOB: THAT'S RIGHT!

CLIFTON: Hey Bob. What about you?

BOB: Am I a living thing? Let's see. I need water. I grow. And, I have parents. That means I'm a living thing.

ALL: THAT'S RIGHT!

 From *Nonfiction Readers Theatre for Beginning Readers* by Anthony D. Fredericks. Westport, CT: Teacher Ideas Press.

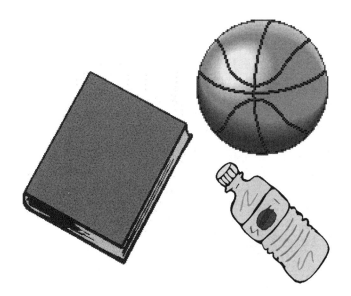

This Is Hard!

(Liquids, Solids, and Gases)

DISCIPLINE

Physical science

SCIENCE CONTENT STANDARD

Properties of objects and materials

SUMMARY

Liquids, solids, and gases are not physical properties that youngsters think about quite often. However, they can begin to comprehend the physical world when they are able to assign objects to 1 of these 3 groups. Putting things into groups is one of the most important steps in understanding the world of science.

PROPS

Three props are needed for this script: a book, a bottle of water, and a basketball (or some other ball that must be filled with air).

PRESENTATION SUGGESTIONS

Invite youngsters to stand around a table on which the 3 props have been placed. They may wish to lay their scripts on the table or hold them in their hands. Be sure that the students are behind the props so that the audience can see them clearly.

EXPERIMENT/ACTIVITY

Here is one of my all-time favorite demonstrations, which I frequently use to illustrate the concepts of liquids, solids, and gases:

Materials

clear plastic or glass container

7-Up™ or other lemon-lime soda

box of raisins

Procedure

Place the clear container in the middle of a table. Gather the students around the table. Pour the 7-Up into the container until it is about ½ inch from the top. Explain to students that you just put a liquid (7-Up) into a solid (container).

Drop 7 or 8 raisins into the liquid (tell students that you are now placing several solids into the liquid). At this point you may wish to ask them to make a prediction about what will happen to the raisins.

Results

Several of the raisins will begin to rise to the surface of the liquid. When they reach the top they will fall back down to the bottom again. The cycle will then repeat itself over and over again.

Explanation

When the raisins are put into the lemon-lime soda, bubbles of carbon dioxide gas begin to adhere to the surface of the raisins. (Incidentally, the more wrinkles the raisins have, the more successful you will be with this activity. I have discovered that Sun Maid® raisins are the best.) The raisins become lighter due to the many bubbles on their surfaces. As a result they float to the top of the liquid. When they get to the surface, all the carbon dioxide bubbles burst, the raisins fall back to the bottom of the container, and the cycle repeats itself.

Make sure students understand that the raisins (and container) are solids, the lemon-lime soda is a liquid, and the (carbon dioxide) bubbles are a gas.

SUGGESTED LITERATURE

Garrett, Ginger. *Solids, Liquids, and Gases*. New York: Scholastic, 2004.

McLuskey, Krista. *The Science of Liquids and Solids*. Milwaukee, WI: Gareth Stevens, 2001.

Simon, Charnan. *Solids, Liquids, Gases*. Mankato, MN: Compass Point Books, 2000.

Stille, Darlene R. *Matter: See It, Touch It, Taste It, Smell It*. Minneapolis, MN: Picture Window Books, 2004.

This Is Hard!

(Liquids, Solids, and Gases)

STAGING: There is no narrator for this script. The 4 characters may stand or may be seated on stools. In front of the characters, place a small table or desk on which you have arranged the 3 primary props.

Anna X		Brad X
	(table)	
Cathy X		Doug X

ANNA: [picks up book] Look at this.

BRAD: Well, silly, it's a book.

ANNA: I know it's a book! But, do you know why it is so special?

BRAD: Because you can read it.

ANNA: No, silly. It's special because it's a solid.

CATHY: What's a solid?

ANNA: A solid is something that takes up space.

DOUG: So, is a bottle of water a solid.

ANNA: Well, the bottle is a solid. Because it takes up space.

DOUG: What about the water?

ANNA: The water is a liquid.

CATHY: What does that mean?

ANNA: Let me see. A solid is something that takes up space.

BRAD: Like a book. Or a rock. Or a table.

ANNA: You're right!

DOUG: But, what about the water?

ANNA: Water also takes up space.

DOUG: So, it's a solid, too?

ANNA: No. A book takes up space. Water takes up space. But they are different.

DOUG: How?

ANNA: That's because a liquid has no shape of its own.

CATHY: A book has its own shape. Right?

ANNA: Right. But water does not have a shape.

DOUG: What does that mean?

ANNA: That means that water is shaped by what it's in. Water has the shape of its container.

CATHY: Can you show me?

ANNA: Sure. Look at this bottle of water [holds the bottle]. See the water inside?

DOUG: Yes.

ANNA: The water has the same shape as the inside of the bottle. If I put the water in another bottle it would have the shape of that bottle.

CATHY: Oh, I see. A book always has the same shape.

DOUG: Right. And water always has the shape of its container.

CATHY: So water is a liquid.

ANNA: Right.

DOUG: And a book, a rock, and a table are solids.

BRAD: What's so special about this basketball.

ANNA: Well, what do you think is inside it?

BRAD: Nothing.

ANNA: No, there's something inside.

BRAD: Really?

ANNA: Sure. What did someone do to blow up the basketball.

BRAD: They put air inside it.

ANNA: So there is air inside the basketball.

BRAD: Oh, I get it. The air is inside the basketball. So, there is something inside.

ANNA: Right. That something is called a gas.

BRAD: So, what is a gas?

ANNA: A gas has no special size. A gas has no special shape. A gas can change size and shape.

BRAD: What else?

ANNA: You cannot smell most gases. You cannot see most gases.

CATHY: O.K., so now we have three things.

ANNA: Some things are solids.

BRAD: Some things are liquids.

DOUG: And some things are gases.

CATHY: Wow! We're scientists now!

It's a Dirty Job

(Our Earth)

DISCIPLINE

Earth science

SCIENCE CONTENT STANDARD

Properties of earth materials

SUMMARY

This script provides students with an introduction to planet Earth. Some of the elements and components of Earth are shared, specifically those with which children are already familiar (mountains, oceans, etc.).

PROPS

Most of the scientists could wear lab coats (borrowed from the local high school). If lab coats are not available, have students each wear a white T-shirt. You may wish to place a globe on a stool in the middle of the staging area. The "scientists" could point to the globe as they deliver their lines.

PRESENTATION SUGGESTIONS

For this script invite the students to stand throughout the presentation. Their placement in the staging area is not critical, and they should feel free to walk around as they say their lines or as others are speaking.

EXPERIMENT/ACTIVITY

Here's an experiment you can use after students have presented the script. It demonstrates how large boulders are broken down into tiny pebbles—by water!

Materials

pieces of sandstone (from a hardware or building supply store)

sealable plastic sandwich bags

water

Procedure

Soak pieces of sandstone in water overnight. The next day, place several pieces of the wet sandstone into sandwich bags and seal them tightly. Place the bags in the freezer overnight. Take them out and examine them the next day.

Results

The sandstone cracks into smaller pieces.

Explanation

When water freezes, it expands. The sandstone absorbs some of the water, taking it up into the air spaces between the sand particles. When the stone was placed in the freezer, the water in it froze and expanded.

In nature, water seeps into the cracks of rocks, freezes in winter, and causes the rocks to break apart. After a while, the rocks are reduced to very small pebbles and eventually to sand.

SUGGESTED LITERATURE

Haugen, David M. *Earth*. San Diego: KidHaven Press, 2002.

Karas, Brian. *On Earth*. New York: G.P. Putnam's Sons, 2005.

Martin, Bill, Jr., and Michael Sampson. *I Love Our Earth*. Watertown, MA: Charlesbridge, 2006.

It's a Dirty Job

(Our Earth)

Es un trabajo sucio (nuestra Tierra)

STAGING: The narrator stands in back and to the side of the other characters. The other characters may stand or move about the staging area. If a globe is used, it should be placed in the middle of the 4 scientists.

Narrator	Scientist 1		Scientist 2
X	X		X
		(globe)	
	Scientist 3		Scientist 4
	X		X

NARRATOR: Welcome to the earth [points]. The earth is round. It is shaped like a ball.

EL NARRADOR(A): Bienvenidos a la Tierra [señalando]. La Tierra es redondeada. Tiene una forma como una pelota.

SCIENTIST 1: The earth looks like a giant marble. The blue is the water. The brown is the land.

EL CIENTÍFICO(A) 1: La tierra parece como una canica. La parte azul es el agua. La parte café es la tierra.

SCIENTIST 2: The land is made of rock and soil. Some rocks are big. Some rocks are small. Rocks come in many shapes.

EL CIENTÍFICO(A) 2: La Tierra es de roca y suelo. Algunas rocas son grandes. Algunas rocas son pequeñas. Las rocas tienen muchas formas.

SCIENTIST 3: The land is not the same in all places. In some places the land is low. In some places the land is high.

EL CIENTÍFICO(A) 3: La Tierra no es la misma en todos los lugares. En algunos lugares, la tierra es baja. En algunos lugares, la tierra es alta.

SCIENTIST 4: Yes. In some places there are hills. In some places the land is flat.

EL CIENTÍFICO(A) 4: Sí. En algunos lugares, hay colinas. En algunos lugares, la tierra es plana.

NARRATOR: What about the water?

EL NARRADOR(A): ¿Y el agua?

SCIENTIST 1: There is a lot of water on the earth. Most of the water is in the oceans. Some water is in lakes and rivers.

EL CIENTÍFICO(A) 1: Hay mucha agua en la Tierra. La gran parte del agua está en los océanos. Hay alguna agua en los lagos y los ríos.

SCIENTIST 2: Some places are covered with ice.

EL CIENTÍFICO(A) 2: Algunos lugares están cubiertas de hielo.

NARRATOR: What is ice?

EL NARRADOR(A): ¿Qué es el hielo?

SCIENTIST 2: Ice is made of water. Ice is water that has frozen. There is also water in the clouds. Sometimes it falls as rain.

EL CIENTÍFICO(A) 2: El hielo es de agua. El hielo es agua helado. Hay agua en las nubes, también. A veces, cae en la forma de lluvia.

SCIENTIST 3: Yes. Water can also be used by people. People need water to drink. People use water to move things. People use water to have fun.

EL CIENTÍFICO(A) 3: Sí. Los seres humanos pueden usar el agua también. Los seres humanos necesitan el agua para beber. Los seres humanos usan el agua para mover las cosas. Los seres humanos usan el agua para divertirse.

SCIENTIST 4: Sometimes water can be harmful. Sometimes water causes floods. A flood is when there is too much water somewhere. Floods can be dangerous.

EL CIENTÍFICO(A) 4: A veces, el agua puede ser peligrosa. A veces, el agua causa las inundaciones. Una inundación es cuando hay demasiada agua en un lugar. Las inundaciones pueden ser peligrosas.

SCIENTIST 1: Water can break down rocks. Water can make rocks smaller. Water can turn rocks into pebbles. Water can turn pebbles into dirt.

EL CIENTÍFICO(A) 1: El agua puede romper las rocas. El agua puede hacer las rocas más pequeñas. El agua puede cambiar las rocas en guijarros. El agua puede cambiar los guijarros en polvo.

NARRATOR: The earth has land. The earth has water. What else does the earth have?

EL NARRADOR(A): La Tierra tiene tierra. La Tierra tiene agua. ¿Qué más tiene la tierra?

From *Nonfiction Readers Theatre for Beginning Readers* by Anthony D. Fredericks. Westport, CT: Teacher Ideas Press. Copyright © 2007 by Anthony D. Fredericks.

SCIENTIST 2: Air. Air covers the earth. We cannot see air. We cannot taste air. But the air is always there.

EL CIENTÍFICO(A) 2: El aire. El aire cubre la Tierra. No podemos ver el aire. El aire no tiene sabor. Pero, el aire siempre está.

SCIENTIST 3: People need air to live. People use air to dry their clothes. People use air to move things. People use air to have fun.

EL CIENTÍFICO(A) 3: La gente necesita el aire para vivir. La gente usa el aire para secar la ropa. La gente usa el aire para mover las cosas. La gente usa el aire para divertirse.

SCIENTIST 4: But air can be dangerous.

EL CIENTÍFICO(A) 4: Pero, el aire puede ser peligroso.

NARRATOR: How?

EL NARRADOR(A): ¿Cómo?

SCIENTIST 1: Air can be harmful. Sometimes air moves very fast. It can make a storm. A storm can be dangerous for people.

EL CIENTÍFICO(A) 1: El aire puede ser peligroso. A veces, va rápidamente. Puede causar una tormenta. Una tormenta puede ser peligrosa a la gente.

SCIENTIST 2: Air can also get dirty. Dirty air can hurt people. People don't like dirty air.

EL CIENTÍFICO(A) 2: El aire también puede ensuciarse. El aire sucio puede hacer daño a la gente. A la gente no le gusta el aire sucio.

NARRATOR: So, there are three parts to the earth. There is the land.

EL NARRADOR(A): Entonces, hay tres partes de la Tierra. Hay la tierra.

SCIENTIST 3: There is the water.

EL CIENTÍFICO(A) 3: Hay el agua.

SCIENTIST 4: And, there is the air.

EL CIENTÍFICO(A) 4: Y, hay el aire.

High Above

(Looking at the Sky)

DISCIPLINE

Space science

SCIENCE CONTENT STANDARD

Objects in the sky

SUMMARY

The script offers an introduction to objects in the sky, specifically the sun, moon, and stars. It capitalizes on what students have seen previously and adds some new information. (NOTE: Caution students that they should NEVER look directly at the sun. To do so would be injurious to their eyes. Invite them to use photographs instead.)

PROPS

No props are necessary for this readers theatre script.

PRESENTATION SUGGESTIONS

Students will be standing throughout the presentation. Encourage them to move around the staging area (although this is not required). You may wish to have students sit on stools or chairs throughout the presentation.

EXPERIMENT/ACTIVITY

Here's an activity that will help students appreciate the relative size of the sun in relationship to the earth.

Materials

bagel

long piece of string

Procedure

Take the children out to the playground or a large field. Take a long piece of string and create a circle on the ground that is 27 feet in diameter (colored yarn may be easier for students to see). Place the bagel on the ground along one edge of the circle. Tell students that the bagel represents the earth and that the string represents the size of the sun.

Results

The "sun" (circle of string) will appear to be considerably larger than the "earth" (bagel).

Explanation

An average bagel is about 3 inches in diameter. When it is placed inside the circle its size relative to the circle of string is considerably smaller. That's because the sun is about 108 times larger than the earth. The circle of string is also 108 times larger than the bagel beside it.

SUGGESTED LITERATURE

Branley, Franklyn Mansfield. *The Sun: Our Nearest Star*. New York: HarperCollins, 2002.

Branley, Franklyn Mansfield. *What the Moon Is Like*. New York: HarperCollins, 2000.

Gibbons, Gail. *The Moon Book*. New York: Holiday House, 1998.

Turnbull, Stephanie. *Sun, Moon, and Stars*. Tulsa, OK: Usborne Publishing, 2003.

High Above

(Looking at the Sky)

STAGING: There is no narrator for this script. The characters can be standing around in any sequence they wish. From time to time they may wish to look and/or point upward at imaginary objects above them (this is optional).

Person 1 X	Person 2 X
Person 3 X	Person 4 X

PERSON 1: I like mornings.

PERSON 2: Why?

PERSON 1: Because that's when the sun comes up.

PERSON 3: Does the sun come up every day?

PERSON 1: Sometimes.

PERSON 4: Sometimes there are clouds. The clouds hide the sun.

PERSON 1: Yes, the sun is hidden. But it's still there.

PERSON 2: Does the sun stay up all day?

PERSON 4: Yes. It is always there.

PERSON 1: We may not see it, but it is always there.

PERSON 2: Then, what happens?

PERSON 4: The sun sets at night.

PERSON 3: What does that mean?

PERSON 1: The sun goes down. The sky gets darker. Soon, we cannot see the sun.

PERSON 2: Why is the sun there?

PERSON 4: The sun gives us light. And, the sun gives us heat.

PERSON 1: Without the sun, we could not live.

PERSON 4: The earth gets warm from the sun, and . . . .

PERSON 1: . . . the earth gets light from the sun.

PERSON 2: What happens at night?

PERSON 4: The sky looks different.

PERSON 1: The moon is in the sky.

PERSON 4: It is smaller than the sun. But, it looks as big as the sun.

PERSON 3: Does the moon have light like the sun?

PERSON 1: No, the moon gets light from the sun.

PERSON 4: The light bounces off the moon. We see the light that bounces off the moon.

PERSON 2: Why does the moon sometimes look different?

PERSON 3: Yeah, why is that?

PERSON 1: Because the moon moves around the earth. When it moves, so does the light.

PERSON 4: Do you want to know something cool?

PERSON 3: Yeah.

PERSON 4: People have walked on the moon, They picked up rocks. And, they brought the rocks back to earth.

PERSON 3: Cool!

PERSON 1: Scientists know that the moon has no water. It has no air. It has high mountains. It has deep craters.

PERSON 2: Wow! That's cool!

PERSON 4: At night there are stars in the sky, too.

PERSON 1: Stars are like the sun. They make their own light. Some stars are big. Some stars are small. The sun is a star. But, stars are further away from us than the sun is.

PERSON 3: Are stars close to us?

PERSON 4: No, stars are far away.

PERSON 1: Yes, they are far, far away.

PERSON 2: There is a lot to learn about the sky.

PERSON 3: You are right. There is a lot in the sky.

PERSON 4: I think there is a lot in our heads, too!

Look at Me!

(Growing and Changing)

DISCIPLINE

Life science

SCIENCE CONTENT STANDARD

Personal health

SUMMARY

Here students are introduced to the concept of "growing and changing." Youngsters are often unaware of the rapid changes that are happening physically to their bodies. They often take growth and development for granted. This script provides an opportunity for you to discuss the health and nutrition needs that help ensure optimum growth and development.

PROPS

No props are necessary for this script.

PRESENTATION SUGGESTIONS

Invite the 2 characters to stand throughout this presentation. They can read their scripts from music stands or appropriately placed desks.

EXPERIMENT/ACTIVITY

This simple activity will help children appreciate the growth and development that has already occurred in their bodies as well as that yet to come.

Materials

old clothes

newsprint

markers

Procedure

Obtain several samples of old or discarded clothing. Be sure to obtain clothes for babies, young children, teenagers, and adults. These items can be obtained from your own family members, relatives, neighbors, thrift stores, Goodwill Industries, Salvation Army stores, flea markets, yard sales, or tag sales.

Post a large sheet of newsprint on one wall of the classroom. Divide it into 3 columns. Label the columns "What I Wore," "What I Wear," and "What I Will Wear."

Mix up the various clothing items in a large cardboard box. Ask students (in small groups) to each select 1 item from the box. Invite them to determine its appropriate placement in 1 of the 3 aforementioned groups. As each group makes its selection, write a brief description of the selected item in the appropriate column. Repeat this with all the other items in the box.

Results

Students will see that items of clothing can be sorted into specific groups according to the growth and development of individuals.

Explanation

As we grow and develop as individuals, we need to change the size of the clothing we wear. Students will be amazed to see the size of clothing they used to wear as well as the sizes of clothing that they may wear in the future. They will appreciate the growth and development process as a lifelong event in their lives.

SUGGESTED LITERATURE

Bradenberg, Aliki. *I'm Growing*. New York: HarperCollins, 1992.

Curtis, Jamie Lee. *When I Was Little: A Four-Year-Old's Memoir of Her Youth*. New York: HarperCollins, 1995.

Look at Me!

(Growing and Changing)

STAGING: There is no narrator for this script. There are only 2 actors. The actors may stand (with their scripts on a desk or table in front of them) or they may be seated on stools or chairs.

Teri	Jerry
X	X

TERI: Hi, Jerry.

JERRY: Hi, Teri.

TERI: Well, what do you know?

JERRY: I'm getting old.

TERI: What do you mean?

JERRY: Today's my birthday.

TERI: Happy Birthday!

JERRY: Thank you. But I'm still getting old.

TERI: What do you mean?

JERRY: Well, my body is changing.

TERI: How do you know?

JERRY: I'm getting taller. That means my bones are growing. It also means that I grow out of my clothes. Every time I grow my parents must buy me new clothes.

TERI: What else?

JERRY: My muscles are growing, too. I know because I can throw a ball further. I can also lift heavy things.

TERI: How do you know?

JERRY: Because I'm stronger. I can carry heavy things.

TERI: What else is happening?

JERRY: My teeth are changing.

TERI: How are your teeth changing?

JERRY: Some teeth are coming out. New teeth are coming in.

TERI: Hey, my teeth are changing, too.

JERRY: I guess you're changing . . . just like me.

TERI: Hey, I bet you're right.

JERRY: I know I'm right.

TERI: How do you know that?

JERRY: Well, look. Your hair is longer.

TERI: You're right. And, you know what?

JERRY: What?

TERI: My clothes are different.

JERRY: How do you know?

TERI: My mother had to buy me new shoes. They were bigger than my old shoes.

JERRY: So, you have big feet [laughs].

TERI: Yes, I do. But, you do too [laughs].

JERRY: I think we are both growing.

TERI: Yes. And we are both changing.

JERRY: Yes. We are both growing and changing.

TERI: You know what?

JERRY: What?

TERI: I think we will always grow. And, I think we will always change.

JERRY: I think you're right.

TERI: [points to audience] And, I think everyone there will grow.

JERRY: [points to audience] And, I think everyone there will change.

TERI: That's right! Everybody grows and . . .

JERRY: . . . everybody changes!

We're All Together

(Families Together)

DISCIPLINE

Friends and family

SOCIAL STUDIES CONTENT STANDARD

Individual development and identity

SUMMARY

"Family" is another concept that children often take for granted. However, it's important for students to understand that there is no such thing as an "average" family. The so-called nuclear family is a distinct minority in this country. Children should have a sense of familial pride—no matter what the composition of their family is.

PROPS

There are no props for this script.

PRESENTATION SUGGESTIONS

Invite children to be seated for this presentation. The narrator may be seated or may be standing in front of a music stand with her or his script.

EXPERIMENT/ACTIVITY

Here is an interesting activity you may wish to share with your students at the conclusion of this readers theatre script.

Materials

newsprint

overhead projector

marker

safety scissors

colored pencils

water colors

Procedure

For each student, tape a sheet of newsprint on a wall of the classroom or library. Place a child between the paper and the light from an overhead projector so that a silhouette of the child's head is projected onto the newsprint. Trace the silhouette on the paper. Do this for each student in the class (you may wish to spread this part of the activity over a period of several days).

Encourage students to cut out their individual silhouettes and write specific details about their families on the paper. They may wish to include the names of family members, places the family travels to, games the family plays, food family members like to eat, or any other aspect of their personal family lives.

Afterward, they can highlight the silhouettes with a watercolor wash and hang them in an appropriate place in the classroom or library. Encourage students to add additional items or events to their silhouettes throughout the year. You may wish to plan special occasions during which students can share their silhouettes with you or each other.

Results

Each student will have her or his own special family remembrance.

Explanation

Students will sense that there are a wide variety of family types, even in a single classroom. Be sensitive to family situations that may be uncomfortable or incomprehensible (e.g., an incarcerated family member, a recent death) to young students. Plan your sharing times accordingly.

SUGGESTED LITERATURE

Kerley, Barbara. *You and Me Together: Moms, Dads, and Kids Around the World*. Washington, DC: National Geographic, 2005.

Kuklin, Susan. *Families*. New York: Hyperion, 2006.

Morris, Ann. *Families*. New York: HarperCollins, 2000.

We're All Together

(Families Together)

STAGING: This script has 1 narrator and 6 characters. The characters can all be seated on stools or chairs in a semicircle in the staging area.

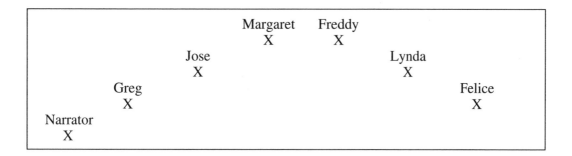

NARRATOR: Good afternoon. Welcome. We are here to talk about families. First, a question. What is a family?

GREG: A family is a mother and a father and some children.

JOSÉ: Not always. Sometimes there might be a grandmother.

MARGARET: Or a grandfather.

FREDDY: Or an aunt.

LYNDA: Or an uncle.

FELICE: Or lots of other relatives.

NARRATOR: Hmmm! It looks like a family can be many things.

GREG: That's right.

JOSÉ: A family can have different people.

MARGARET: It can have lots of people . . . .

FREDDY: . . . or few people.

LYNDA: Families come in all shapes . . . .

FELICE: . . . and sizes.

NARRATOR: I guess you're right.

GREG: Sometimes a family can be small.

JOSÉ: Like a husband and a wife.

MARGARET: Or a mother and a daughter.

FREDDY: Or a mother and a son.

LYNDA: Or a father and a daughter.

FELICE: Or a father and a son

NARRATOR: I guess families can be big.

GREG: Yes. They can be very big.

JOSÉ: with lots of children . . .

MARGARET: . . . and lots of grandparents . . . .

FREDDY: . . . and lots of aunts and uncles . . . .

LYNDA: . . . and lots of cousins . . . .

FELICE: . . . and lots of other people. People you may not know.

NARRATOR: So, I guess you were right. Families come in all shapes. And they come in all sizes.

GREG: They also do lots of special things.

JOSÉ: Families go on trips.

MARGARET: Families go to the movies.

FREDDY: Families go to the store.

LYNDA: Families share stories together.

FELICE: And, families eat ice cream together.

NARRATOR: So, there are different kinds of families. And, families do different kinds of things.

GREG: But, don't forget . . . .

JOSÉ: Yes, don't forget . . . .

MARGARET: Families do one more thing . . . .

FREDDY: Yes, they do one more thing together . . . .

LYNDA: It's the most important . . . .

FELICE: Yes, it's the most important.

NARRATOR: Well, what is it?

ALL: They LOVE each other!

Pals

(My Friends)

DISCIPLINE

Friends and family

SOCIAL STUDIES CONTENT STANDARD

Individual development and identity

SUMMARY

This script provides students with a brief introduction to the concept of friendship. Many students mistakenly believe that friendship is something that just "happens." However, it's important for youngsters to understand that people engage in certain acts or behaviors that produce and enhance friendships.

PROPS

The narrator can have an imaginary or make-believe microphone. You may wish to use a real microphone (unplugged) or create one on your own (e.g., a corncob stuck on the end of a short dowel).

PRESENTATION SUGGESTIONS

During the performance of this script all the characters should be standing. They can each have their own music stands (to hold scripts) or can stand in front of desks on which their scripts are placed. Be sure the narrator stands to the side of each individual as the separate interviews are being conducted.

EXPERIMENT/ACTIVITY

This is a simple activity youngsters can participate in over a period of several days.

Materials

sheet of newsprint

markers

Procedure

Using a marker, divide the newsprint into 4 sections. In the top left-hand section write the words "At School." In the bottom left-hand section write the words "At Home." In the top right-hand section write the words "On the Playground." In the bottom right-hand section write the words "On Vacation."

Invite students to brainstorm about various kinds of jobs that need to be done in each of the locations printed on the chart. For example, for "At Home" students might suggest washing dishes or raking leaves. For "At School" students might suggest emptying trash or cleaning chalkboards. Invite children to suggest as many possibilities as they can for each of the 4 sections.

After a sufficient quantity of items has been suggested, invite students to revisit the chart. Ask them to tell you the jobs that could be done better or faster if 2 friends were working together. Use a different color marker to check off the jobs that 2 friends could accomplish more efficiently together.

Results

There will be many check marks across all 4 sections of the chart.

Explanation

Afterward, take time to discuss the different types of everyday jobs that friends could do together. Emphasize the fact that we are happier and more productive when we make and keep friends. Good friends are important to good relationships and good work.

SUGGESTED LITERATURE

Bunnett, Rochelle. *Friends at School*. Long Island City, NY: Star Bright Books, 2006.

Pals

(My Friends)

STAGING: The narrator is the only character who moves in this presentation. She or he can have a make-believe microphone and move from person to person as though each is being interviewed separately.

	Amanda	Peter	LaToya
	X	X	X
Narrator			
X			

NARRATOR: Good morning. Today we want to talk with some people. May I talk to you?

AMANDA: Yes, what do you want to know?

NARRATOR: Well, can you tell me what a friend is?

AMANDA: Sure. A friend is someone who helps you.

NARRATOR: What do you mean?

AMANDA: A friend helps you pick up toys. A friend helps you do a job. A friend helps you when you are sad.

NARRATOR: So, a friend will always help you.

AMANDA: Yes.

NARRATOR: Tell me more.

AMANDA: Friends like to help friends.

NARRATOR: So, if you help someone, you can be their friend?

AMANDA: That's right.

NARRATOR: Thank you very much [moves to next person]. Tell me, what is a friend?

PETER: A friend will listen to you.

NARRATOR: I don't understand.

PETER: A friend listens quietly. A friend hears what you say.

NARRATOR: So, if I listen to what you say, I could be your friend?

PETER: That's right. Good friends always listen.

NARRATOR: What does a good listener do?

PETER: A good listener looks at the person speaking. A good listener doesn't talk. A good listener pays attention.

NARRATOR: If I listen to you, I could be your friend.

PETER: Yes, you could. I like when someone listens to me.

NARRATOR: I like when someone listens to me, too.

PETER: Then, I guess we could be friends.

NARRATOR: That would be nice.

PETER: I think that would be great!

NARRATOR: Thank you [turns to next person]. What is a friend to you?

LATOYA: A friend is someone who always smiles at you.

NARRATOR: When someone smiles, they could be your friend?

LATOYA: That's right. Friends always smile.

NARRATOR: If I am sad, will you smile at me.

LATOYA: Of course. I would like to be your friend.

NARRATOR: Thank you. Thank you for smiling.

LATOYA: You're welcome. I like smiling at people.

NARRATOR: That must mean you have a lot of friends.

LATOYA: I guess so. Because friends always smile at friends.

NARRATOR: So, when people smile, they can be friends?

LATOYA: Yes.

NARRATOR: Well, I've learned a lot. I know that friends help friends. I know that friends listen to friends. And, I know that friends laugh together, and play together, and have a good time together.

ALL: That's right!

NARRATOR: Will you be my friends?

ALL: YES!

Where I Learn

(Our School)

DISCIPLINE

Friends and family

SOCIAL STUDIES CONTENT STANDARD

Individuals, groups, and institutions

SUMMARY

This script touches on a very familiar topic for kids: school. It makes the point that school is an important place to be, simply because there is a lot to learn and learning is something important in all our lives.

PROPS

This script can be performed with minimal props. Each of the students' desks could have a variety of school supplies on them, or you may wish to have nothing on each desk.

PRESENTATION SUGGESTIONS

Ask the students to sit during this presentation. Their scripts can be lying on the desks. Invite them to look at each other when they are speaking.

EXPERIMENT/ACTIVITY

Invite each student to go home and interview 1 or 2 older members of her or his family. Invite youngsters to gather as much information as possible about school in "the good old days." What were some of the things their parents or grandparents learned long ago? What did their school look like? How many students went to the school?

If possible, invite students to gather information about their parents' or grandparents' recollections about first grade. Perhaps relatives have some mementos, artifacts, or photos from those early years. Invite youngsters to gather together as many of those items as possible (each one should have a small tag affixed to indicate its owner).

Provide each student with a shallow cardboard box (similar to a cake box, which you can obtain at your local bakery). Invite students to arrange their artifacts into a pleasing display. Label each item with a brief description or date. When each box is completed, place a sheet of plastic wrap over each one so that each looks like a miniature museum display case. Arrange the boxes on a table or shelf in the classroom and invite students to look at the artifacts brought in by their classmates.

You may wish to spend a little time talking about how education has changed over the years. You may wish to discuss customs, games, teaching styles, subjects, how people dress, etc. This would also be a good opportunity to share some photos or thoughts about your own schooling, something kids are always delighted to hear about.

SUGGESTED LITERATURE

Ajmera, Maya. *Back to School*. Minneapolis, MN: Sagebrush, 2002.

Where I Learn

(Our School)

Dónde Aprendo (Nuestra Escuela)

STAGING: The narrator stands in front and to the side of all the characters. The 3 main characters are sitting at desks in a loose semicircle. You may wish to have 1 or 2 books on each desk along with a collection of school supplies (pencil, paper, crayon box, etc.).

```
                                      Tim
                                       X
                          Tom                      Tammy
                           X                         X
            Narrator
               X
```

NARRATOR: Welcome to our school. School is fun. School is cool! We learn new things here. Let's listen.

EL NARRADOR(A): Bienvenidos a nuestra escuela. La escuela es divertida. La escuela es fantástica. Aprendemos cosas nuevas aquí. Escuchemos.

TOM: Boys and girls go to school.

TOMÁS: Los chicos y las chicas asisten a la escuela.

TIM: Teachers go to school, too.

TIMOTEO: Los maestros van a la escuela, también.

TAMMY: Every day busses bring boys and girls to school.

TAMMY: Cada día, los autobuses llevan a los chicos y las chicas a la escuela.

TOM: Everybody goes to a classroom.

TOMÁS: Todas las personas van a la sale de clase.

TIM: A classroom is a special place. It's where people learn.

TIMOTEO: Una sale de clase es un lugar especial. Es donde las personas aprenden.

TAMMY: Do teachers learn, too.

TAMMY: ¿Aprenden los maestros, también?

TOM: Yes, they do. They have to go to school before they can be a teacher.

TOMÁS: Sí, aprenden. Tienen que asistir a la escuela para hacerse un maestro.

TIM: What do they learn?

TIMOTEO: ¿Qué aprenden?

TAMMY: They learn how to teach. And, they learn how to jump rope.

TAMMY: Aprenden a enseñar. Y, aprenden a saltar a la comba.

TOM: Are you kidding me?

TOMÁS: ¿En serio?

TAMMY: No, they have to learn many new things.

TAMMY: No, tienen que aprender muchas cosas nuevas.

TOM: We learn, too. We learn how to read. We learn how to add. We learn how to subtract. We learn about animals. We learn about plants.

TOMÁS: Nosotros aprendemos, también. Aprendemos a leer. Aprendemos a sumar. Aprendemos a restar. Aprendemos sobre los animales. Aprendemos sobre las plantas.

TIM: Wow, that's a lot to learn.

TIMOTEO: ¡Vaya! Eso es mucho para aprender.

TAMMY: When we learn all that, we get smart.

TAMMY: Cuando aprendemos todo eso, nos ponemos listos.

TOM: Just like our teacher!

TOMÁS: Es igual que nuestro maestro.

TIM: That's right. The more we learn, the smarter we get.

TIMOTEO: Correcto. Cuanto más aprendemos, lo más inteligentes nos hacemos.

TAMMY: Do we learn how to jump rope?

TAMMY: ¿Aprendemos nosotros a saltar a la comba?

TOM: I think so. We learn other games, too.

TOMÁS: Pienso que si. Aprendemos otros juegos, también.

TIM: A lot happens at school.

TIMOTEO: Mucho pasa en la escuela.

TAMMY: That's right. School is cool!

TAMMY: Exacto. ¡La escuela es fantástica!

ALL: School is cool! School is cool! School is cool!

TODOS: ¡La escuela es fantástica! ¡La escuela es fantástica! ¡La escuela es fantástica!

PART II
READING LEVEL, SECOND GRADE

Flower Power

(How Plants Grow)

DISCIPLINE

Life science

SCIENCE CONTENT STANDARD

Life cycles of organisms

SUMMARY

Children are always fascinated by growing things—especially plants. This script introduces them to seed plants. The germination process is highlighted along with the 3 essential parts of a new plant: roots, leaves, and stem.

PROPS

No props are necessary for this script. If desired, you may wish to provide the "Seed" with paper "leaves" to hold during the presentation.

PRESENTATION SUGGESTIONS

The "Seed" will begin the presentation in a crouching position and eventually work her or his way into a fully extended standing position. The narrator and 3 characters can all be standing or could be sitting on stools.

EXPERIMENT/ACTIVITY

This is one of my favorite plant activities, simply because it effectively demonstrates the "ingredients' necessary for seed germination.

Materials

36 radish seeds

6 plastic sandwich bags

paper towels (cut in half)

water

candle wax

marker

Procedure

Invite students to moisten pieces of paper towel and place them in the bottom of sandwich bags as directed below. Drop 6 radish seeds in each bag (leave the bags open). Label each bag with a number and then finish setting up each bag as follows:

- Bag 1: paper towel, water, no light (put in a drawer or closet), room temperature

- Bag 2: paper towel, water, light, room temperature

- Bag 3: paper towel, no water, light, room temperature

- Bag 4: no paper towel (seeds floating in water), light, room temperature

- Bag 5: paper towel, water, no light, keep in refrigerator or freezer

- Bag 6: paper towel, no water, no light, room temperature, seeds covered with candle wax

Invite students to record the date and time they begin this activity and check each of the bags twice daily for changes.

Results

Eventually, students will note that the seeds in Bag 1 and Bag 2 begin to germinate. There may be some minor change in the seeds in Bag 4.

Explanation

Discuss with students the fact that seeds need favorable temperature, adequate moisture, and oxygen to germinate. Light is not needed for germination.

SUGGESTED LITERATURE

Branigan, Carrie. *How Plants Grow*. Mankato, MN: Smart Apple Media, 2005.

Helbrough, Emma. *How Flowers Grow*. Tulsa, OK: Usborne Publishing, 2003.

Royston, Angela. *How Plants Grow*. Chicago: Heinemann Library, 2001.

Scrace, Carolyn. *Growing Things*. New York: Scholastic, 2002.

Spilsbury, Louise A., and Richard Spilsbury. *How Do Plants Grow?* Chicago: Heinemann Library, 2005.

Flower Power

(How Plants Grow)

STAGING: There are 4 speaking parts and 1 nonspeaking part ("Seed") in this script. The narrator can stand at the back and to the side of the 3 speaking characters. The "Seed" should be placed in the front and center of the staging area.

```
                                              Narrator
                                                 X
                         Person 2
                            X
            Person 1                   Person 3
               X                          X
                         "Seed"
                            X
```

NARRATOR: Good morning. We are standing in a garden. Three people are talking. They are talking about a seed. They want to plant the seed. They want something to grow. The seed is waiting to be planted.

[The "seed" should crouch down into a tight ball. She or he should have her or his arms wrapped around her or his knees.]

PERSON 1: Well, I think we should plant our seed.

PERSON 2: I know that we can get a plant to grow from the seed.

PERSON 3: A seed is very special.

PERSON 1: That's because a seed has a tiny plant in it.

PERSON 2: A seed also has something else.

PERSON 3: A seed also has some food for the new plant.

[The "seed" should move 1 hand in a slow upward motion above her or his head.]

PERSON 1: Look [points to seed]. The tiny plant is beginning to grow.

PERSON 2: What is making it grow?

PERSON 3: It is using the food inside of the seed.

PERSON 1: It has just enough food to get started.

[The "seed" moves her or his other hand up and out. She or he lifts her or his head in an upward motion. She or he rises up to a semicrouching position—hands above her or his head.]

PERSON 2: Look. Now the tiny plant is growing some more.

PERSON 3: We should remember that this seed is underground.

PERSON 1: That's right. The seed is doing all this growing under the soil.

PERSON 2: Wow. The seed is breaking open. Roots are going down into the soil.

PERSON 3: The roots are important for the new plant.

PERSON 1: The roots help the plant get water.

PERSON 2: The roots help the plant get food.

[The "seed" begins to "unfold" some more. Rising from a semicrouching position, she or he spreads her or his legs apart. She or he raises her or his hands high above her or his head. The body is still not fully extended.]

PERSON 3: Look. Now there are leaves.

PERSON 1: You're right. The leaves move up and out of the soil.

PERSON 2: The leaves are important, too. They help the new plant get sunlight.

PERSON 3: Let's not forget the stem. The stem is important, too.

From *Nonfiction Readers Theatre for Beginning Readers* by Anthony D. Fredericks. Westport, CT: Teacher Ideas Press. Copyright © 2007 by Anthony D. Fredericks.

PERSON 1: You're right. The stem supports the new plant.

[The "seed" is now fully extended. Arms are raised high into the air. The body is erect. The legs are straight and spread apart.]

PERSON 2: Look. It's a new plant.

PERSON 3: It has roots that go into the soil. The roots get water. The roots get food for the plant.

PERSON 1: And the new plant has leaves. The leaves get sunlight. They also help the new plant grow.

PERSON 2: And the new plant has a stem. The stem holds the plant. The water up the stem. So does the food.

PERSON 3: Wow! Look, there is a brand new plant. There is a brand new plant. It grew from a tiny seed.

Terrible Lizards

(Dinosaurs)

DISCIPLINE

Life science

SCIENCE CONTENT STANDARD

Organisms and environment

SUMMARY

With this script students will be introduced to the incredible world of dinosaurs. Long a popular topic with youngsters of all ages, this presentation will provide students with some basic information that can be supplemented by the myriad books on the topic. Be sure to follow up with a range of supplemental literature from the school library.

PROPS

Since the story revolves around a conversation among members of a family, there are no special props necessary. If you like, obtain an illustration or photograph of a dinosaur and have it posted behind the players. Or you might wish to have students create a collage of dinosaur pictures to arrange behind the players.

PRESENTATION SUGGESTIONS

Students should be standing throughout this script. They may wish to hold their scripts in their hands, or you can provide music stands for them. Inform them that they will be taking on the roles of selected family members and that they may wish to use the tone of voice or speech patterns of family members with which they are most familiar.

EXPERIMENT/ACTIVITY

Here's a brief activity appropriate for use upon completion of the script. It will help students appreciate the enormous size of selected dinosaurs.

Materials

ball of string or a skein of yarn

Procedure

Cut the string or yarn into several lengths, as indicated below. Take each length of string or yarn out to the playground. Lay each one on the ground and inform students that the length of a certain piece of string represents the length of a selected dinosaur. Invite students to walk the length of each piece of string to appreciate the respective sizes of the selected dinosaurs. Use the following:

Velociraptor	8 feet
Allosaurus	25 feet
Stegosaurus	28 feet
Triceratops	30 feet
Tyrannosaurus Rex	40 feet
Apatosaurus	70 feet
Ultrasaurus	100 feet

Results

Students will begin to appreciate the variations in dinosaur size as well as the lengths of some of the largest "terrible lizards."

Explanation

Dinosaurs came in all shapes and sizes. In fact, most of the dinosaurs were about the size of chickens. However, the most "popular" ones are those that elicit the most "ooo's and "ahhhhh's"—that is, the long, tall, and heavy ones. The fact that some of these "monsters" were carnivores gives them even greater stature in the eyes of children. That's irrespective of the fact that most dinosaurs were actually herbivores.

SUGGESTED LITERATURE

Birch, Robin. *Meat-eating Dinosaurs*. Broomall, PA: Chelsea Clubhouse, 2003.

Gibbons, Gail. *Dinosaur Discoveries*. New York: Holiday House, 2005).

Kelsey, Elin. *Finding Out About Dinosaurs*. New York: Firefly Books, 2000.

Markle, Sandra. *Outside and Inside Dinosaurs*. New York: Atheneum, 2000.

Zoehfeld, Kathleen Weidner. *Dinosaurs Big and Small*. New York: HarperCollins, 2002.

Terrible Lizards

(Dinosaurs)

Los lagartos terribles (los dinosaurios)

STAGING: The narrator stands in front and to the side of the other characters. The other characters should stand in one place in the staging area. The players may wish to glance at any posted pictures throughout the reading of the script.

Mother X	Father X	
Brother X	Sister X	Narrator X

NARRATOR: Once upon a time there were dinosaurs. There were no people. There were no buildings. There were no cities. Just lots of dinosaurs.

EL NARRADOR(A): Érase una vez en que había los dinosaurios. No había personas. No había edificios. No había ciudades. Sólo muchos dinosaurios.

FATHER: Some dinosaurs were smaller than cats. Some dinosaurs were larger than elephants. Dinosaurs came in all shapes and sizes. Animals today come in all shapes and sizes.

EL PADRE: Algunos dinosaurios eran más pequeños que los gatos. Algunos dinosaurios eran más grandes que los elefantes. Los dinosaurios eran de todas formas y tamaños. Hoy en día, los animales son de todas formas y tamaños.

MOTHER: Dinosaurs ate different things. Some dinosaurs ate plants. Some dinosaurs ate meat.

LA MADRE: Los dinosaurios comían varias cosas. Algunos comían plantas. Algunos comían carne.

BROTHER: Did dinosaurs ever eat hamburgers?

EL HERMANO: ¿Comieron alguna vez las hamburguesas?

SISTER: No, silly.

LA HERMANA: No, tonto.

MOTHER: Some dinosaurs had sharp teeth. They used their teeth to attack other animals. Sometimes they wanted to eat. And, sometimes they wanted to protect themselves.

LA MADRE: Algunos dinosaurios tenían dientes afilados. Usaban los dientes para atacar a otros animales. A veces, querían comer. Y algunas veces, querían protegerse.

FATHER: There were lots of different dinosaurs.

EL PADRE: Había muchos dinosaurios diferentes.

NARRATOR: Scientists learn about dinosaurs all the time. Some scientists think dinosaurs lived in a warm climate. Other scientists think dinosaurs lived where it was cool. Scientists don't always agree. That's what makes science so interesting.

EL NARRADOR(A): Los científicos aprenden sobre los dinosaurios todo el tiempo. Algunos científicos creen que los dinosaurios vivieron en lugares cálidos Otros científicos creen que los dinosaurios vivieron en lugares frescos. Los científicos no siempre están de acuerdo. Por esta razón, la ciencia es tan interesante.

FATHER: Most large dinosaurs moved very slowly. That's because they were very heavy.

EL PADRE: La mayoría de los dinosaurios grandes movían lentamente. Eso es porque eran muy pesados.

MOTHER: Yeah, and they ate lots of plants. They had to eat lots and lots of plants. They had big stomachs.

LA MADRE: Sí, y comían muchas plantas. Tenían que comer muchísimas plantas. Tenían estómagos grandes.

BROTHER: But, what did the small dinosaurs eat?

EL HERMANO: Pero, ¿qué comían los dinosaurios pequeños?

MOTHER: Small dinosaurs ate small animals or eggs.

LA MADRE: Los dinosaurios pequeños comían animales pequeños o huevos.

BROTHER: Do you think they ate fried eggs?

EL HERMANO: ¿Piensas que comían huevos fritos?

SISTER: Don't be so silly. Of course, they didn't eat fried eggs. They had to find the eggs of small animals.

LA HERMANA: No seas tonto. Claro que no, no comían los huevos fritos. Tenían que hallar los huevos de los animales pequeños.

FATHER: Here's something I learned. Most dinosaurs had flat teeth, not sharp teeth.

EL PADRE: Aquí es algo que aprendí. La mayoría de los dinosaurios tuvieron dientes desafilados, no afiliados.

BROTHER: Why was that?

EL HERMANO: ¿Por qué fue así?

MOTHER: I can answer that. It's because they ate lots of plants. They used their flat teeth to grind their food. Horses eat plants. They have flat teeth, too.

LA MADRE: Puedo contestar eso. Es porque comían muchas plantas. Usaban los dientes desafilados para masticar su comida. Los caballos comen plantas. Tienen dientes planos, también.

BROTHER: Yeah, but I bet horses never ate dinosaurs!

EL HERMANO: Sí, pero apuesto a que los caballos nunca comieron los dinosaurios.

SISTER: There you go—getting silly again!

LA HERMANA: Otra vez, eres tonto.

NARRATOR: One of the largest dinosaurs was 130 feet long. That's longer than three school buses parked in a row. It weighed more than 12 elephants

EL NARRADOR(A): Uno de los dinosaurios más grandes era 130 pies de largo. Es más largo que tres autobuses en una fila. Tenía un peso de más de 12 elefantes.

FATHER: Wow, that's really, really big!

EL PADRE: ¡Vaya! ¡Es muy grande!

MOTHER: You're not kidding that's big.

LA MADRE: De verdad, eso es grande.

SISTER: So, what happened to all the dinosaurs?

LA HERMANA: Entonces, ¿qué pasó a todos los dinosaurios?

MOTHER: Nobody is sure. Scientists have different ideas. One thing for sure, learning about dinosaurs is lots of fun. I bet we could find some cool books in the library.

LA MADRE: Nadie sabe. Los científicos tienen varias ideas. Una cosa segura, para aprender sobre los dinosaurios es muy divertida. Estoy segura que encontramos libros interesantes en la biblioteca.

FATHER: Well. Let's go!

EL PADRE: Pues, ¡Vamános!

It's Hot, It's Bright!

(Light and Heat)

DISCIPLINE

Physical science

SCIENCE CONTENT STANDARD

Light, heat, electricity, and magnetism

SUMMARY

Light and heat are often difficult concepts for children to understand simply because they are more abstract than concrete. This script will introduce your students to these 2 concepts in a humorous way. Plan several exposures to the topics of "heat and light" to ensure adequate comprehension.

PROPS

No props are necessary for this script. If you wish, you may borrow some lab coats from your local high school for the characters to wear.

PRESENTATION SUGGESTIONS

For this script invite youngsters to sit on stools or in chairs throughout the presentation. They should address their comments and remarks to each other in voices loud enough for members of the audience to hear.

EXPERIMENT/ACTIVITY

Here is an activity that can be used as one of several in your unit on "heat and light." (Note: This is a teacher demonstration only.)

Materials

wire coat hanger

wire cutters

small candle

2 wooden blocks (same size)

5 wire paper clips

Procedure

Using the wire cutters, cut the straight bottom section of a wire coat hanger. Lay the wire on a table. Light the candle and drip wax onto 5 different spots on the wire. Each time, quickly press a wire paper clip onto the wax so that the paper clips adhere to the length of wire coat hanger. Blow out the candle

Lay the wire across the two wooden blocks as in the diagram below. Place the candle underneath one end of the wire length. Light the candle so that the end of the wire is in the flame.

Invite students to observe what happens to the paper clips.

————————— * —————— * —————— * —————— * —————— * —————————
                      ☐   ☐   ⇧

————— = length of wire coat hanger
* = paper clip
☐ = wooden block
⇧ = candle

Results

One by one the paper clips will begin to fall off the wire.

Explanation

Heat travels through some objects better than others. It travels through metal very well. When you place the end of the wire into the candle flame, the wire becomes hot. The molecules in the wire are heated and the heat is quickly transferred from one molecule to the next. That heat passes down the length of the wire. As it does it heats the candle wax. As the wax is heated it becomes a liquid and loosens its "grip" on each paper clip. As a result, each paper clip falls off the wire separately.

SUGGESTED LITERATURE

Trumbauer, Lisa. *All About Heat*. New York: Scholastic, 2004.

Trumbauer, Lisa. *All About Light*. New York: Scholastic, 2004.

Walker, Sally M. *Heat*. Minneapolis, MN: Lerner Publications, 2005.

It's Hot, It's Bright!

(Heat and Light)

STAGING: The narrator stands in the back and to the side of the other characters. The other characters may be standing or seated on stools.

	Narrator X			
Ashley X	Carrie X	Maria X	Inez X	

NARRATOR: Welcome to Science Class. Right here [points to characters] we have four young scientists. They are learning new things. Today they are learning about heat. And, they are learning about light. Let's listen.

ASHLEY: You know, sometimes when I'm inside I get really hot.

CARRIE: So do I.

MARIA: I do too. But, sometimes I get hot when I'm outdoors.

INEZ: Yes, so do I. I guess "heat" is everywhere.

ASHLEY: You're right. I heard that heat was energy.

CARRIE: Yeah. I heard that heat was really energy in motion.

MARIA: How does that work?

INEZ: Well, let's say you are frying some eggs.

ASHLEY: I wouldn't do that. My mother is the one who cooks.

CARRIE: Yeah, me too. Except when she goes on a trip. Then my dad has to cook. Ugh. He's not a good cook.

ASHLEY: Yeah, once my dad tried to cook some oatmeal. It really tasted bad because he burned it.

CARRIE: Yeah, some Dad's aren't very good cooks.

INEZ: Anyway, you are cooking some eggs. The frying pan gets hot.

MARIA: I know. The frying pan gets hot because the heat moves from the stove to the pan.

INEZ: Yes, and then the heat moves from the pan to the food.

ASHLEY: Then, the eggs start to cook.

CARRIE: Or start to burn if your dad is cooking them.

MARIA: Yeah, then the heat moves into the air near the pan.

INEZ: So, heat is something that moves through objects.

ASHLEY: I know. It moves through some objects better than other objects.

CARRIE: I know that it moves through metal really well. That's why my mom has to use a pot holder to hold the pan. She doesn't want to burn herself.

MARIA: Hey, that's cool.

CARRIE: No, really, that's very hot!

MARIA: Well, I have a question. Is heat the same thing as light?

INEZ: Well, yes and no.

MARIA: Yes and no. What do you mean?

INEZ: Well you see, light is a kind of energy. Remember that heat is a kind of energy, too.

ASHLEY: I know. Light can come from many things. Let's see if we can think of some.

CARRIE: Light comes from the sun.

INEZ: And light can come from a fire.

MARIA: And light can come from a lightbulb.

ASHLEY: You are all right. Some things can make light. But, many other things cannot make light.

CARRIE: O.K., so what else do we know?

INEZ: Well, my dad told me that light from a lamp moves in a straight line. He said that when you turn on a lamp the light goes everywhere.

ASHLEY: My dad said that if you are sitting near a light, the light goes straight to a book you are reading.

MARIA: My dad said that light can go through some things. It can go through windows. He said that light doesn't go through other things, like walls.

CARRIE: Hey, I guess our dads are pretty smart.

INEZ: Yes, they are!

Water, Water Everywhere

(Water)

DISCIPLINE

Earth science

SCIENCE CONTENT STANDARD

Properties of earth materials

SUMMARY

Water, water everywhere. Water is one of those elements we all take for granted. It's always been there and we assume that it always will be. This brief script introduces youngsters to 2 types of water—fresh and salt. The script would be most appropriate as an introduction to a larger unit on water.

PROPS

No props are necessary for this script. After the reading of this script and as appropriate, you may wish to mix 1 or 2 teaspoons of salt into a pitcher of water. Pour a small amount into each of several small cups. Invite children to dip their tongues into a separate and individual cup of the salt water to taste it. (Note: Caution students not to swallow the water.)

PRESENTATION SUGGESTIONS

Students should be seated on stools or chairs for this presentation. Their placement in the staging area is not critical, and you are free to adjust their placements as necessary.

EXPERIMENT/ACTIVITY

Here's one of my favorite "water" activities—one that will help children appreciate the use of wells to obtain necessary groundwater.

Materials

cardboard tube (toilet roll)

large coffee can

sand

aquarium or potting gravel

water

Procedure

Place the tube upright in the middle of the coffee can. Holding the tube, pour a layer of about 1½ inches of gravel on the bottom of the coffee can around the outside of the tube. Pour a second layer, this time of sand, on top of the gravel (until the level of sand is about 1 to 2 inches below the top of the tube).

Slowly pour some water onto the sand until the water reaches the top of the sand. Invite students to notice what happens inside the tube.

Results

After a short time, water begins to rise inside the tube.

Explanation

When it rains, groundwater collects under the surface of the earth. This collected water can be very shallow or deep depending on the rock formations and kind of soil in a particular area. Because there is a limit to the amount of water that can collect in an area, water pressure builds up in these underground "lakes." If a well has been dug nearby, the pressure forces water into it where it can be reached and used.

SUGGESTED LITERATURE

Ampt, Peter. *Fresh Water*. Broomall, PA: Chelsea House, 2001.

Davies, Nicola. *Oceans and Seas*. Boston: Houghton Mifflin, 2004).

Gray, Samantha. *Ocean*. New York: DK Publishing, 2001.

Simon, Seymour. *Oceans*. New York: HarperCollins, 2006.

Water, Water Everywhere

(Water)

STAGING: There is no narrator for this script. The 4 characters can be seated on stools or chairs.

	Vicky X	Julie X	
Mark X			Mike X

MARK: You know, I was reading about water in a library book.

VICKY: O.K., what did you learn?

MARK: I learned that most of the earth is covered by water.

JULIE: Wow, that's cool. That must be a lot of water.

MIKE: Yes, it is. I heard that more than three-fourths of the earth has water on it.

VICKY: That doesn't leave a lot of room for the land.

MIKE: No, it doesn't.

MARK: But, did you know that there are two kinds of water.

JULIE: Two kinds! Let's see. Isn't one kind of water called fresh water?

MIKE: That's right. Fresh water is the water in rivers and streams.

VICKY: Yes, and fresh water is the water in rain and snow.

JULIE: Lakes also have fresh water.

MARK: Here's something amazing. Most fresh water is locked up.

JULIE: What do you mean "locked up?"

MARK: Well, most fresh water is locked up in icebergs.

MIKE: You mean those big giant things at the South Pole?

MARK: Right!

VICKY: And there are icebergs at the North Pole, too.

MIKE: But, there is also lots of fresh water in the ground, too.

VICKY: Right. Most of the water in the ground comes from rain and snow.

MARK: When water is in the ground it's called "groundwater."

VICKY: Well, duh!

MARK: Hey, smarty pants, do you know why groundwater is important?

JULIE: Hey, yourself. I know why it's important. Lots of people get their drinking water from the ground.

MIKE: That's right. They dig wells and pump the water up.

VICKY: But, there's something else that's amazing about water.

MARK: What's that?

VICKY: Most of the water in the world is salt water. It's called salt water because it has lots of salt in it.

JULIE: That means that fresh water doesn't have salt.

MIKE: Right!

VICKY: Wait! I know. Most of the salt water in the world is in oceans.

MIKE: Right again!

VICKY: It's the oceans that cover three-fourths of the earth.

MIKE: Right! Right! Right!

JULIE: So, we know that there is lots of fresh water.

MIKE: And, we know there is lots of salt water.

MARK: Yes, there's water, water everywhere

VICKY: Water in the lakes

Water in the sea.

Some is for the little fish,

And some is for me!

Weather, or Not!

(Weather)

DISCIPLINE

Earth science

SCIENCE CONTENT STANDARD

Changes in the earth and sky

SUMMARY

This script introduces youngsters to 3 basic elements of weather—clouds, rain, and snow. Students receive specific information on how clouds are formed and how they contribute to the production of rain and snow.

PROPS

You may wish to use a large cardboard box that has been cut into the size and shape of a TV screen. The weatherperson can stand (or sit) behind the box (in full view of the audience) and pretend that she or he is a TV meteorologist. You may wish to have students view 2 or 3 videorecordings of the local news and the evening weather report before performing this script.

PRESENTATION SUGGESTIONS

The weatherperson should be standing (preferably in front of a map of the United States or world). The other 4 characters can be seated in small chairs.

EXPERIMENT/ACTIVITY

Here's a demonstration that will help students understand water vapor. PLEASE NOTE: This is a teacher demonstration. Students should NOT handle any of the items during or after the demonstration.

Materials

> 1 large pot
>
> 1 small pot
>
> ice cubes
>
> water

Procedure

Fill the large pot about halfway with water and place it on the stove or a hot plate. Bring the water to a boil. Place a tray full of ice cubes in the small pot. Hold the small pot (using kitchen gloves) over the steam rising from the boiling pot.

Results

The cold surface of the upper pot cools the steam rising from the boiling water in the lower pot. The steam changes back into water in the form of drops. As the drops get larger and heavier, they begin to fall as "rain."

Explanation

The boiling water is just like the water in oceans and lakes that is being heated by the sun. The steam is just like the water that evaporates into the air as water vapor. As the water vapor rises it begins to cool. As it cools it forms into tiny droplets. These tiny droplets form into larger drops. When they become too heavy, they fall in the form of rain.

SUGGESTED LITERATURE

Adams, Simon. *The Best Book of Weather*. New York: Kingfisher, 2001.

Berger, Gilda, and Melvin Berger. *Hurricanes Have Eyes But Can't See and Other Amazing Facts About Wild Weather*. New York: Scholastic, 2004.

Mack, Lorrie. *Weather*. New York: Dorling Kindersley, 2004.

Michaels, Pat. *W Is for Wind: A Weather Alphabet*. Chelsea, MI: Sleeping Bear Press, 2005.

Seymour, Simon. *Weather*. New York: HarperCollins, 2006.

Weather, or Not!

(Weather)

¡El tiempo, si, o no! (El pronóstico)

STAGING: The narrator in this play takes on the role of a TV weatherperson. That individual should be standing in front of a map of the United States, much as a weatherperson would be on a local TV news program. The other characters take on the roles of family members who are watching the local news. They may be seated in chairs facing a cardboard box cut into the shape of a TV screen.

```
                        Weatherperson
                             X
                           (box)
        Mom                                 Dad
         X                                   X

      Grandpa                             Grandma
         X                                   X
```

WEATHERPERSON: Welcome to the 6:00 news. First, let's look outside. Let's look at the weather. First, you'll see [points] lots of clouds.

EL METEORÓLOGO(A): Bienvenidos a las noticias de 6:00. Primero, vamos a mirar afuera. Miremos el tiempo. Primero, se ven [señalando] muchas nubes.

GRANDMA: Hey, please help me. I can't remember. What's a cloud?

LA ABUELA: Oye, por favor, ayúdame. No recuerdo. ¿Qué es una nube?

GRANDPA: Well, dear, there are different kinds of clouds.

EL ABEULO: Pues, querida, hay diferentes tipos de nubes.

MOM: Right, Pa. Some clouds are all white and puffy.

LA MADRE: Sí, Papá. Algunas nubes son blancas e hinchadas.

DAD: Just like big fat marshmallows. Just like the ones I like to eat when we camp.

EL PADRE: Son como esponjas grandes y gordos. Como los que me gusta comer cuando acampamos.

GRANDPA: You're right, son. But, some clouds are thick and dark.

EL ABUELO: Tienes razón, hijo. Pero algunas nubes son gruesas y oscuras.

MOM: They look like giant sponges filled with water.

LA MADRE: Parecen como esponjas gigantes llenas de agua.

GRANDPA: Right you are. Clouds can all look different. But, they are all made in the same way.

EL ABUELO: Tienes razón otra vez. Las nubes pueden parecer diferentes. Pero, son del mismo material.

GRANDMA: How's that?

EL ABUELO: ¿Cómo es eso?

MOM: Well, clouds are made of small drops of water. Every day the sun heats up water. It heats the water in oceans, lakes, rivers and ponds.

LA MADRE: Pues, las nubes son hechas de gotas pequeñas de agua. Cada día, el sol calienta el agua. Calienta el agua de los océanos, los lagos, los ríos, y los estanques.

From *Nonfiction Readers Theatre for Beginning Readers* by Anthony D. Fredericks. Westport, CT: Teacher Ideas Press. Copyright © 2007 by Anthony D. Fredericks.

GRANDPA: Yeah, and then something really neat happens.

EL ABUELO: Sí, y después, algo muy especial ocurre.

GRANDMA: I remember now. Evaporation happens. Evaporation is when water changes into water vapor.

LA ABUELA: Ahora me acuerdo. La evaporación ocurre. La evaporación es cuando el agua cambia al vapor.

DAD: Hey, now we're on a roll. Water vapor is something you can't see. Water vapor is invisible. Because it's not heavy it moves up into the sky. As it moves higher it gets colder.

EL PADRE: Oye, no paramos. El vapor es algo que no se puede ver. El vapor es invisible. Como no pesa, sube al cielo. Como sube más alto, se enfría.

GRANDMA: That's because it's cold way up in the sky.

LA ABUELA: Eso es porque hace frío muy alto en el cielo.

GRANDPA: Hey, I think Grandma's got it now

EL ABUELO: Oye, pienso que la abuela entiende ahora.

GRANDMA: You bet I do! Then, the water vapor changes. It changes into very tiny droplets of water. All that water together makes up a cloud.

LA ABUELA: ¡Claro que sí! Entonces, todo el vapor cambia. Cambia en gotitas de agua. Toda esa agua hace una nube.

WEATHERPERSON: Folks, we've been watching all these clouds. And it looks like its going to rain. It should rain for several days. So, be sure to take an umbrella along. We could have lots of wet, rainy days ahead.

EL METEORÓLOGO(A): Señores y señoras, hemos estado mirando todas estas nubes. Y parece que va a llover. Debe llover por algunos días. Entonces, lleven un paraguas. Es posible que tengamos muchos días húmedos y de lluvia en el futuro.

DAD: O.K., can someone help me out. What exactly is rain? I can't remember.

EL PADRE: Bueno, ¿alguien puede ayudarme? ¿Qué es la lluvia exactamente? No recuerdo.

GRANDMA: I can help. You see, all those tiny drops of water get together in a cloud. When they do, they move around and bump into each other. The drops get larger and larger.

LA ABUELA: Yo puedo ayudar. Ves, todas esas gotitas de agua se juntan en una nube. Cuando están juntas, se mueven y se chocan. Las gotitas se hacen cada vez más grandes.

GRANDPA: Yeah, it's like baking a cake. You keep adding more and more ingredients. When you do the cake gets bigger and bigger.

EL ABUELO: Sí, es como hacerse una tarta en el horno. Agrega más y más ingredientes. Cuando haces esto, la tarta se hace cada vez más grande.

MOM: O.K., let's get back to the rain. When those big drops get together they get very heavy. So, then they fall out of the clouds as rain. If there is a lot, then we have a lot of rain.

LA MADRE: Bueno, regresemos a la lluvia. Cuando esas gotas grandes se reúnen, pesan muchas. Entonces, se caen de las nubes como lluvia. Si hay muchas, entonces, tenemos mucha lluvia.

WEATHERPERSON: Look. The mountains will get something other than rain. It looks like snow. I hope people have their snow shovels ready!

EL METEORÓLOGO(A): Mira. Las montañas van a recibir algo más que lluvia. Parece como nieve. Espero que las personas estén listas con sus palas de nieve.

DAD: Remember that winter a few years back? The one where we got lots and lots of snow?

EL PADRE: ¿Se acuerdan de ese invierno hace algunos años? ¿El invierno en que recibimos muchísima nieve?

GRANDPA: I sure do. And, I sure do remember one thing. We had to shovel all that snow off the driveway.

El ABUELO: Claro que sí. Y, me acuerdo también de una cosa. Tuvimos que mover quitar toda esa nieve de la entrada con pala.

MOM: So, let's think about snow. Anybody remember what it is?

LA MADRE: Entonces, pensemos en la nieve. ¿Alguien recuerda qué es?

GRANDMA: I do. Sometimes, there are clouds very high in the sky. Those clouds are where the air is very, very cold. Those clouds have water drops and bits of ice in them.

LA ABUELA: Yo recuerdo. A veces, hay nubes que están muy altas en el cielo. Esas nubes son donde el aire es muy frío. Esas nubes son hechas de gotas de agua y pedazos de hielo.

GRANDPA: Yeah, and those bits of ice and water drops bump into each other. When they do, they get bigger and bigger. When they get too heavy, they fall out of the clouds as snow.

EL ABUELO: Sí, y esos pedazos de hielo y gotas de agua se chocan. Cuando se chocan, crecen y crecen. Cuando están demasiado pesados, se caen de las nubes en la forma de nieve.

DAD: There's one more thing you can't forget.

EL PADRE: Hay otra cosa más que tienen que recordar.

GRANDMA: Right! The air under the clouds has to be cold, too. If it is, the falling snow doesn't melt. It stays on the ground. Or, it stays on the driveway until someone with a shovel takes it away.

LA ABUELA: ¡Sí! El aire que está debajo de las nubes tiene que estar frío, también. Si está frío, la nieve que cae no se derrite. Se queda en el suelo. O, se queda en la entrada hasta que alguien la quita con pala.

GRANDPA: Like me.

EL ABUELO: Como yo.

WEATHERPERSON: So, that's the weather for today. Make sure you have an umbrella if it rains. Make sure you have a shovel if it snows. Oh, and don't forget to have a nice weekend. Bye for now.

EL METEORÓLOGO(A): Entonces, ese es el pronóstico para hoy. Recuerden de su paraguas si hay lluvia. Recuerden de su pala si hay nieve. ¡Ah! Y no se olviden de tener un buen fin de semana. Adiós por ahora.

Taking Care of Me

(Keeping Healthy)

DISCIPLINE

Human body

SCIENCE CONTENT STANDARD

Personal health

SUMMARY

Students need to understand, from an early age, that good health doesn't just happen. It is part of a concentrated effort by the individual and her or his family members. When children begin to understand the essential ingredients of good health, they can begin making lifestyle decisions that will help ensure a lifetime of good health.

PROPS

There are no specific props for this script. It would be advantageous to provide each character with a prominent sign indicating her or his title/name (e.g., Miss Sleep).

PRESENTATION SUGGESTIONS

Each of the characters should be seated on a stool or chair. The narrator (Mr. Body) talks to each of the characters individually. After a character has spoken it is not necessary for her or him to exit the staging area.

EXPERIMENT/ACTIVITY

The following activity will help sensitize children to some of the elements of a healthy lifestyle. Please feel free to modify or adjust these charts in accordance with the needs of individual students in your class.

Materials

charts (see below)

markers

Procedure

Duplicate the charts below. You may wish to make individual charts for each child. Or, you may elect to construct an oversize series of charts for all the members of the class. Another option would be to post these charts in the classroom and record elements of your healthy lifestyle for class observation and discussion.

Exercise

Day	Minutes
Monday	
Tuesday	
Wednesday	
Thursday	
Friday	
Saturday	
Sunday	

Sleep

Day	Hours
Monday	
Tuesday	
Wednesday	
Thursday	
Friday	
Saturday	
Sunday	

Water

Day	Glasses
Monday	
Tuesday	
Wednesday	
Thursday	
Friday	
Saturday	
Sunday	

Results

Results will vary.

Explanation

Depending on how you set up this activity, students will see that individuals vary in the amount of exercise, sleep, and water they get every day or every week. Inform students that these variations are normal. It's more important that students' averages over time are equivalent to the following:

- Exercise—30–45 minutes per day

- Sleep—10–11 hours per day

- Water—7–8 glasses per day

SUGGESTED LITERATURE

Petrie, Kristin. *The Food Pyramid*. Edina, MN: ABDO Publishing, 2004.

Salzmann, Mary Elizabeth. *Getting Enough Sleep*. Edina, MN: ABDO Publishing, 2004.

Salzmann, Mary Elizabeth. *Keeping Your Body Clean*. Edina, MN: ABDO Publishing, 2004.

Sears, Martha, R.N., and William Sears, M.D. *Eat Healthy, Feel Great*. New York: Little, Brown, 2002.

Thomas, Pat. *My Amazing Body: A First Look at Health and Fitness*. Hauppauge, NY: Barrons, 2002.

Taking Care of Me

(Keeping Healthy)

STAGING: In this script the characters are the elements necessary for a healthy lifestyle. The narrator is a human body (male or female) who is seeking information about maintaining good health. The characters can all be standing at individual music stands or seated on stools.

	Mr. Food X	Miss Exercise X
Narrator (Mr. Body) X		
	Miss Sleep X	Mr. Water X

NARRATOR (MR. BODY): Hi, my name is Mr. Body. I'm the narrator for this story. I'm also a student. I want to learn more about myself. I want to learn how to stay healthy. I don't like getting sick. I want to grow up healthy. I want to grow up strong.

MR. FOOD: Well, hey, Mr. Body, we can help you.

MR. BODY: Tell me, what should I do?

MR. FOOD: Well, you need lots of me. I mean you need lots of good food.

MR. BODY: Why is that?

MR. FOOD: That's because good food helps you stay healthy.

MR. BODY: Really? What else does it do.

MR. FOOD: Good food helps you play. It helps you work. And, it helps you learn.

MR. BODY: Wow! That's really cool.

MR. FOOD: But, you have to eat the right kind of me. I mean, you have to eat the right kinds of food.

MR. BODY: Please tell me.

MR. FOOD: You have to eat dairy products like milk and cheese. You have to eat vegetables like carrots and beans. You have to eat meat, poultry, and fish. You have to eat fruit like apples and peaches. And, you have to eat breads and cereals.

MR. BODY: Wow, that's a lot to eat. I'm really not very hungry right now.

MR. FOOD: You don't have to eat all that at the same time. You have to eat some of those each day.

MISS EXERCISE: Hey, don't forget me.

MR. BODY: What can you do for me?

MISS EXERCISE: You need lots of me. That is, you need lots of exercise every day.

MR. BODY: Why?

MISS EXERCISE: Good exercise helps you stay healthy. Exercise helps make strong muscles.

MR. BODY: Hey, I'm strong already.

MISS EXERCISE: O.K., but if you want to stay strong, you need to exercise every day.

MR. BODY: Every day?

MISS EXERCISE: Yes, every day. That will help keep your heart healthy. It will help keep your lungs healthy. It will help keep your whole body healthy.

MR. BODY: O.K., what else do I need to do?

MISS SLEEP: You need lots of me.

MR. BODY: Oh, really!

MISS SLEEP:	Yes, really. You need rest and sleep to stay healthy. Sleep helps your body work better. Sleep also helps your body feel better.
MR. BODY:	Well, that sounds good. Anything else?
MISS SLEEP:	Yes, you are still growing. So you need about 10 or 11 hours of sleep every day.
MR. BODY:	Wow, that's a lot.
MISS SLEEP:	You're right, it is a lot. But you could get sick if you don't sleep enough.
MR. BODY:	[pointing to Mr. Water] I guess I need you, too.
MR. WATER:	You are right.
MR. BODY:	Why do I need you?
MR. WATER:	Water helps your body work. Water helps keep you healthy.
MR. BODY:	How much do I need?
MR. WATER:	You need about 8 glasses of water every day.
MR. BODY:	8 glasses! That's a lot!
MR. WATER:	Yes it is. But it will help you work better. It will help you think better. It will help you play better. And . . .
MR. BODY:	. . . and, it will help me stay healthy.
MR. WATER:	Right!
MR. BODY:	To stay healthy I need four friends.
MR. FOOD:	You need me!
MISS EXERCISE:	You need me!
MISS SLEEP:	You need me!
MR. WATER:	And, you need me!
MR. BODY:	To stay healthy, I need all four of my friends.

Hip, Hip, Hooray!

(The Fourth of July)

DISCIPLINE

History

SOCIAL STUDIES CONTENT STANDARD

Time, continuity, and change; Power, authority, and governance; Civic ideals and practices

SUMMARY

Everybody loves a parade! And everybody loves fireworks—especially all the fireworks that are set off each July 4. While children are also active participants in the picnics, outings, and celebrations associated with our nation's birthday, they may not always realize the roots of those celebrations. This script provides them with some important insights.

PROPS

Each of the reporters can be provided with a simply constructed (and imaginary) microphone.

PRESENTATION SUGGESTIONS

The "president" should be seated in a large chair (if possible). The reporters can all be standing at individual music stands or desks.

EXPERIMENT/ACTIVITY

Here's a quick and easy activity I have used many times to help youngsters appreciate the significance of July 4 as the birthday of the United States.

Materials

several birthday cards (new or used)

safety scissors

adhesives

photocopied birth announcements

Procedure

You can do this particular activity in 1 of 2 ways. First, obtain a number of new or used birthday cards (these can be borrowed from friends, neighbors and relatives). Cut off the front part of several selected cards and hand them out to students. Invite students (as individuals or in small groups) to create a "birthday card" for the United States.

Tell them that they have the front of the card, but that the "insides" of the card were lost. Encourage them to create a saying, statement, or sentence for the inside of each card front that would honor or celebrate this nation's birthday.

An alternate way of approaching this activity would be to provide students with several examples of photocopied birth announcements (again, tap into the largesse of your friends, neighbors, and relatives). After students have reviewed several examples, invite them to create a "birth announcement" for the United States. What are the "vital statistics" (e.g., Mother = England, Father = colonists, length = 13 colonies long, etc.)?

Create an appropriate area in the classroom or library for students to display their work.

Results

Students will create a variety of birthday greetings for the United States.

Explanation

Students will understand the "connection" between the birthday of our country and the celebrations on July 4.

SUGGESTED LITERATURE

Douglas, Lloyd G. *Let's Get Ready for Independence Day*. New York: Children's Press, 2003.

Marx, David F. *Independence Day*. New York: Children's Press, 2001.

Murray, Julie. *Independence Day*. Edina, MN: ABDO Publishing, 2005.

Nelson, Robin. *Independence Day*. Minneapolis, MN: Lerner Publications, 2003.

Sanders, Nancy I. *Independence Day*. New York: Children's Press, 2003.

Hip, Hip, Hooray!

(The Fourth of July)

STAGING: This script has 4 newspaper reporters and the president of the United States. Provide each of the reporters with an imaginary microphone (wrap a ball of modeling clay around the top of a pencil).

Reporter 1 X	Reporter 2 X	
		The President X
Reporter 3 X	Reporter 4 X	

REPORTER 1: Excuse me, Mr. President. Can you tell us why this is a special day.

PRESIDENT: Yes. today is the Fourth of July. It's the birthday of the United States.

REPORTER 2: I thought that only people could have birthdays.

REPORTER 3: My cat had a birthday last week.

REPORTER 4: Well, your cat is weird.

PRESIDENT: I'd be happy to explain. You see many years ago . . . .

REPORTER 1: Could you tell us exactly. How many years ago?

PRESIDENT: It was more than 300 years ago.

REPORTER 2: That's a l-o-o-n-n-g-g time ago!

PRESIDENT: Well about 300 years ago people came to America from England. They were called Pilgrims. They lived in 13 different colonies.

REPORTER 3: Could you tell us what a colony is?

PRESIDENT: Of course. A colony is a group of people. They are ruled by a country that is far away. The colonies in America were ruled by England.

REPORTER 4: Didn't England have a king?

PRESIDENT: Yes, England had a king. His name was George.

REPORTER 1: King George, right?

PRESIDENT: Right. Anyway, the people here wanted to rule themselves.

REPORTER 2: Why?

PRESIDENT: They thought England was too far away. They thought England didn't understand them. They thought England didn't know what they needed.

REPORTER 3: But England thought different, didn't it?

PRESIDENT: Yes, they did. They wanted to tell the people in the colonies how to live. Or, what to say.

REPORTER 4: I bet the people in the colonies didn't like that.

PRESIDENT: You're right. So, some leaders all got together. They met in Philadelphia. They met in the summer of 1776.

REPORTER 1: Excuse me, sir. Where is that city?

PRESIDENT: Philadelphia is in Pennsylvania. You can find it on a map. Just look in a corner of the state. That's where Philadelphia is.

REPORTER 2: So, what did the leaders do?

PRESIDENT: They talked about things they didn't like. And they talked about things they liked. At the end they wrote a paper.

REPORTER 3: Did this paper have a name?

PRESIDENT: Yes, it did. It was called the Declaration of Independence.

REPORTER 4: What was in the paper?

PRESIDENT: The Declaration of Independence told England that the colonies wanted to be free.

REPORTER 1: Wow! The people in England must have been mad.

PRESIDENT: Yes, they were. But the leaders in Philadelphia thought that freedom was best.

REPORTER 2: So, then what happened?

PRESIDENT: All the leaders in Philadelphia signed the paper. They were willing to fight England in order to be free.

REPORTER 3: Excuse me, sir. When did they sign the Declaration of Independence?

PRESIDENT: They signed it on July 4, 1776.

REPORTER 4: What did that mean?

PRESIDENT: That meant that we wanted to be free. It meant that we wanted our independence. It meant that we would fight England to get our independence.

REPORTER 1: I bet I can guess. We won the war. It was called the War for Independence.

PRESIDENT: You're right. We were free from England.

REPORTER 2: So, we were an independent country.

PRESIDENT: That's correct. That's why we celebrate every July 4 as the birthday of our country.

ALL: HAPPY BIRTHDAY AMERICA!

HIP, HIP, HOORAY!

HIP, HIP, HOORAY!

HIP, HIP, HOORAY!

The First Thanksgiving

(The Pilgrims of Plymouth)

DISCIPLINE

Holidays and celebrations

SOCIAL STUDIES CONTENT STANDARD

Time, continuity, and change

SUMMARY

This script offers students an opportunity to discover the roots of a favorite American holiday—Thanksgiving. This is done through a description made to a student (Assad) from another country in which Thanksgiving is not practiced.

PROPS

No props are necessary for this script. You may wish to display some illustrations of the first Thanksgiving on the wall behind the players or share illustrations with students at the end of the presentation.

PRESENTATION SUGGESTIONS

For this script, invite the students to stand throughout the presentation. Their placement in the staging area is not critical, and they should feel free to walk around as they say their lines or as others are speaking.

EXPERIMENT/ACTIVITY

Here's an activity students can do after they have performed the readers theatre presentation.

Procedure

Invite students to assemble a collection of "Thanksgiving" books from the school library. Provide each of several small groups with a large sheet of newsprint. Ask each group to divide the newsprint into 2 long columns. Invite each group to list the similarities between the events portrayed in the library books on the left side of each sheet. Students can list any significant differences in the books in the right-hand column on each sheet. You may wish to provide groups with an opportunity to share and compare their various lists. What do they notice? What implications can they draw as a result of any differences? You may wish to get into a discussion about how different people (and different authors) may interpret the same historical event a little differently.

SUGGESTED LITERATURE

Boyce, Natalie Pope, and Mary Pope Osborne. *Pilgrims: A Nonfiction Companion to Thanksgiving on Thursday*. New York: Random House, 2005.

Kamma, Anne. *If You Were at the First Thanksgiving*. New York: Scholastic, 2001.

Penner, Lucille Recht. *The Pilgrims at Plymouth*. New York: Random House Books for Young Readers, 2002.

The First Thanksgiving

(The Pilgrims of Plymouth)

El primer día de acción de gracias
(Los primeros colonos de Nueva Inglaterra)

STAGING: There is no narrator for this script. All of the characters may stand at individual music stands or be seated on stools. They may wish to move around or stay in one place. Make clear to students that "Assad" is a student from another country—a country that has holidays that are different from those celebrated in the United States. In "Assad's" native country there is no Thanksgiving holiday.

```
                        Assad
                          X
              Michael              Sarah
                 X                   X
      Cindy                                  Tyrone
        X                                      X
```

TYRONE: Hey, Assad, welcome to the United States. And, welcome to our class. I think you are going to like it here.

TYRONE: Oye, Assad, bienvenido a los Estados Unidos. Y, bienvenido a nuestra sale de clase. Creo que te gustará estar aquí.

ASSAD: Thank you very much. The United States is a special place. It is very different from the country I grew up in.

ASSAD: Muchas gracias. Los Estados Unidos son un lugar especial. Es muy diferente del país en que yo crecí.

CINDY: How is it different?

CINDY: ¿En qué sentido?

ASSAD: Your buildings all look different. The people who live here wear different kinds of clothes. And, your school is different from the one I used to go to.

ASSAD: Sus edificios parecen diferentes. Las personas que viven aquí llevan diferentes tipos de ropa. Y su escuela es diferente de la escuela a la que asistía.

SARAH: How was your school different?

SARAH: ¿Cómo era diferente su escuela?

ASSAD: I went to a school that had only three rooms. We did not have a blackboard. And, we did not have all the books that you have here.

ASSAD: Asistía a una escuela que sólo tenía tres sales de clase. No teníamos una pizarra. Y no teníamos todos los libros que tienen aquí.

MICHAEL: It sure sounds like it was really different.

MIGUEL: Parece que fue muy diferente.

ASSAD: Yes. I also know that in the United States there are different holidays. There are lots of holidays here.

ASSAD: Sí, y sé también que en los Estados Unidos, hay vacaciones diferentes. Hay muchas vacaciones aquí.

TYRONE: You're right. Holidays help us remember special people. They also help us remember special times in our history.

TYRONE: Tienes razón. Las vacaciones nos ayudan recordar a las personas especiales. También, recuerdan los momentos especiales de nuestra historia.

CINDY: That's right. Holidays are times that everyone celebrates together. When we celebrate we do special things. We do them with our family or with our friends.

CINDY: Eso es correcto. Las vacaciones son ocasiones especiales en que todos celebramos juntos. Cuando celebramos hacemos cosas especiales. Las hacemos con nuestra familia o con nuestros amigos.

ASSAD: Tell me about the holiday you call Thanksgiving.

ASSAD: Háblame sobre las vacaciones que se llaman el día de acción de gracias.

MICHAEL: O.K. You see, many years ago . . . .

MIGUEL: Bueno. Ves, hace muchos años . . . .

SARAH: . . . It was more than 400 years ago.

SARAH: Fue hace más de 400 años.

MICHAEL: That's right. 400 years ago a group of people left England. They sailed across the Atlantic Ocean to come to this land. They were called Pilgrims.

MIGUEL: Eso es correcto. Hace 400 años, un grupo de personas salió de Inglaterra. Cruzaron el Océano Atlántico para llegar a esta tierra. Se llamaron los primeros colonos.

ASSAD: Why did they leave England?

ASSAD: ¿Por qué se fueron de Inglaterra?

TYRONE: They left because the king didn't like their religion. They wanted to practice their religion in a different way. But, the king wouldn't let them. So, they left and came here.

TYRONE: Se fueron porque al rey no le gustaba su religión. Querían practicar su religión en una manera diferente. Pero, el rey no les permitió. Entonces, se fueron y llegaron aquí.

ASSAD: That happens in my country, too. Some people think their religion is best. Other people think their religion is best. Sometime they fight about it.

ASSAD: Ese tipo de cosa ocurre en mi país también. Algunas personas creen que su región es la mejor. Otras personas creen que su religión es la mejor. A veces, tienen discusiones sobre la religión.

CINDY: Well, the pilgrims didn't want to fight. So, they came here.

CINDY: Pues, los primeros colonos no querían tener discusiones. Entonces vinieron aquí.

SARAH: When they got here they discovered Indians living nearby. The Indians were friendly. They taught the Pilgrims how to grow food. They learned how to grow corn and other vegetables.

SARAH: Cuando llegaron, descubrieron que había indígenas que vivían cercas. Fueron amables. Enseñaron a los primeros colonos a cultivar comida. Aprendieron cómo cultivar maíz y otros vegetales.

TYRONE: Then, in the fall they gathered all those vegetables. They were very thankful for all the food they had.

TYRONE: Entonces, en el otoño recogieron todos los vegetales. Estuvieron agradecidos por toda la comida que tuvieron.

MICHAEL: They were so thankful that they all decided to celebrate.

MIGUEL: Estuvieran tan agradecidos que decidieron celebrar.

CINDY: Yeah. The women cooked cornbread and fish stew. It took about three days to cook all the food. The men hunted some turkeys. And the kids gathered berries and nuts.

CINDY: Sí. Las mujeres cocinaron el pan de maíz y el estofado de pescado. Pasaron tres días cocinando toda la comida. Los hombres cazaron pavos. Y los niños coleccionaron bayas y nueces.

SARAH: And, don't forget the Indians. The Indians came, too. They brought some deer meat. They also brought some wild turkeys.

SARAH: Y, no se olviden de los indígenas. Los indígenas vinieron, también. Trajeron alguna carne de ciervo. Además, trajeron pavos salvajes.

MICHAEL: So, everyone sat around and ate all that food. The Pilgrims and Indians ate together. It was a big celebration.

MIGUEL: Entonces, todos se sentaron y comieron toda la comida. Los primeros colonos y los indígenas comieron juntos. Fue una celebración grande.

ASSAD: We have celebrations in my country with lots of food, too.

ASSAD: Tenemos celebraciones en mi país con mucha comida, también.

TYRONE: Well, this celebration was a special one. It was the first Thanksgiving. People were very thankful for the food they had.

TYRONE: Pues, esta celebración fue una celebración especial. Fue el primer día de acción de gracias. La gente estuvo muy agradecida por la comida que comieron.

SARAH: And, we have been celebrating Thanksgiving ever since. It is always the last Thursday in November.

SARAH: Y, hemos estado celebrando el día de acción de gracias entonces. Es siempre el último jueves de noviembre.

CINDY: Yeah, the whole country gives thanks for what we have.

CINDY: Sí, todo el país da gracias por lo que tenemos.

ASSAD: That is very interesting. I like your holiday called Thanksgiving. But, you know what?

ASSAD: Eso es interesante. Me gustan sus vacaciones que se llaman el día de acción de gracias. Pero, ¿sabes algo?

ALL: What?

TODO: ¿Qué?

ASSAD: I am just like the Pilgrims. Because I am thankful to be in the United States. This is my new country.

ASSAD: Soy como los primeros colonos, porque estoy agradecido de estar en los Estados Unidos. Esta es mi nueva patria.

PART III

READING LEVEL, THIRD GRADE

Pollution Solution

(Ecology)

DISCIPLINE

Life science

SCIENCE CONTENT STANDARD

Organisms and environment

SUMMARY

Many youngsters think that the problem of pollution is something that only adults can solve. This script helps them realize that everybody is responsible for the "care and feeding" of the world they live in. Children begin to sense that they (as well as adults) must be vigilant and concerned about maintaining a clean environment. They can also think about how their actions may influence other children (and even adults) to act.

PROPS

There are no props for this script.

PRESENTATION SUGGESTIONS

You may wish to post a few pictures or photographs of various ecosystems (e.g., streams, clouds over mountains, cityscapes, etc.). Take time after the presentation to discuss the global implications of pollution as well as local implications.

EXPERIMENT/ACTIVITY

Here is an activity that will help children appreciate the impact of pollution on specific ecosystems.

Materials

4 small (baby food) jars, without lids

tape and felt-tip marker

aged water (left uncovered to let chlorine gas escape)

pond soil

pond water with scum (algae)

liquid plant fertilizer

liquid detergent

motor oil

vinegar

Procedure

Label the 4 jars "A," "B," "C," and "D." Prepare each jar as follows: fill the jar halfway with aged tap water, put in a ½-inch layer of pond soil, add 1 teaspoon of plant fertilizer, then fill the jar the rest of the way with pond water and algae. Allow the jars to sit on a windowsill or in some other sunny location for 2 weeks.

Next, treat each separate jar as follows:

- Jar "A": add 2 tablespoons of detergent

- Jar "B": add enough motor oil to cover the surface

- Jar "C": add ½ cup of vinegar

- Jar "D": leave as is

Allow the jars to sit for at least 4 weeks.

Results

With the addition of the detergent, motor oil, and vinegar to the first 3 jars, the healthy growth that took place in the jars during the first 2 weeks of the experiment has severely changed. In fact, those jars now probably show little or no growth taking place, while the organisms in jar "D" continue to grow.

Explanation

Detergent, motor oil, and vinegar are pollutants that prevent organisms from obtaining the nutrients and oxygen they need to continue growing. The detergent shows what happens when large quantities of soap are released into an area's water. The motor oil shows what happens to organisms after an oil spill. The vinegar shows what can happen when high levels of acids are added to an ecosystem such as a pond or a stream. When industry, factories, homeowners, and other consumers put these and other kinds of pollutants into streams, rivers, and other sources of water, it can seriously affect and even destroy the plants and animals that live there.

SUGGESTED LITERATURE

Bellamy, Rufus. *Action for the Environment: Clean Air*. Mankato, MN: Smart Apple Media, 2006.

Binns, Tristan Boyer. *Clean Planet: Stopping Litter and Pollution*. Chicago: Heinemann Library, 2005.

Donald, Rhonda Lucas. *Water Pollution*. New York: Children's Press, 2001.

Fredericks, Anthony D. *Near One Cattail: Turtles, Logs, and Leaping Frogs*. Nevada City, CA: Dawn Publications, 2005.

Harlow, Rosie, and Sally Morgan. *Pollution and Waste*. New York: Kingfisher, 2002.

Pollution Solution

(Ecology)

STAGING: There is no narrator for this script. The characters all take on the roles of everyday students. They may be standing or seated on stools.

	Student 2 X	Student 3 X	
Student 1 X			Student 4 X

STUDENT 1: Do you remember when we were at recess today?

STUDENT 2: Yes.

STUDENT 1: Do you remember seeing all the trash that was on the ground?

STUDENT 3: Yes. It was everywhere.

STUDENT 1: I don't understand why people throw trash on the ground.

STUDENT 4: Maybe they just don't care.

STUDENT 2: My father was telling me about people who put chemicals in rivers and streams.

STUDENT 3: Why would people want to do that?

STUDENT 4: Maybe they just don't care. Or maybe they don't understand what they are doing.

STUDENT 1: What kinds of things do they put in the rivers and streams?

STUDENT 2: They put soap in the water. They put trash in the water. They put bad stuff in the water.

STUDENT 3: Then, what happens?

STUDENT 2: All that stuff is bad for the fish. All that stuff is bad for the plants that live by the river. All that stuff is bad for the insects that live by the stream.

STUDENT 4: It would be like someone putting junk in your cereal.

STUDENT 2: You're right! You wouldn't want to eat bad stuff for breakfast. Well, the animals that live in streams and rivers don't want that stuff either.

STUDENT 1: It sure is a dangerous world out there.

STUDENT 3: You're right about that.

STUDENT 4: And, guess what? People also put stuff in the air.

STUDENT 1: Like what?

STUDENT 4: They put dirt and smoke in the air.

STUDENT 1: It seems like humans are always putting bad things onto the land. Or in the water. Or in the air.

STUDENT 2: Yeah, I guess you're right. Maybe some people don't care.

STUDENT 3: Oh, I think people care. Sometimes they don't think about what they're doing. They think one piece of paper won't matter.

STUDENT 4: And, they think that just a some soap in a stream won't matter.

STUDENT 1: Or, they think that a little puff of smoke from a factory won't matter.

STUDENT 2: But, all those things can be harmful for plants and animals.

STUDENT 3: You're right. All that stuff becomes bad when everybody does it. If everybody put just one piece of trash on the ground . . . .

STUDENT 4: . . . or if everybody just put a some soap in a stream . . . .

STUDENT 1: . . . or if everybody just put smoke from their car in the air . . . .

STUDENT 2: . . . yeah, if everybody just added one little thing to the ground or water or air it would be really bad.

STUDENT 3: Yeah, you're right. If millions of people just added little things to the ground, water, and air then it could all be a big, big mess.

STUDENT 4: So, what does that all mean?

STUDENT 2: It means that every person must be careful.

STUDENT 1: It means that every person must watch what they do with their trash.

STUDENT 3: It means that every person must think.

STUDENT 4: I get it. Everybody must work together to be sure our world is clean. Everybody is responsible. Everybody must be careful.

STUDENT 1: The world is for everybody.

STUDENT 2: And everybody must take care of the world.

STUDENT 3: Let's get rid of all the pollution.

STUDENT 4: Yeah, when everybody works together, we can have a pollution solution!

ALL: Yeah, a pollution solution.

STUDENT 1: That's when adults and children all work together.

Round and Round

(Life Cycles)

DISCIPLINE

Life science

SCIENCE CONTENT STANDARD

Life cycles of organisms

SUMMARY

"Life cycles" is a topic important in any study of life science. Students need to understand about the balance of nature. That is, nature is composed of many interlocking cycles that work together to ensure the survival of all species. This script will introduce them to that concept.

PROPS

No props are necessary for this script.

PRESENTATION SUGGESTIONS

For this script students should be seated on stools. The narrator should be placed off to the side since she or he only has 2 short speaking parts. Students may wish to obtain clothing that is emblematic of their respective roles: for example, an apron for Mrs. Mother, a wrench for Mr. Plumber, a dollar bill for Mrs. Banker, etc.

EXPERIMENT/ACTIVITY

The following experiment is one of my all-time favorites because it provides students with an opportunity to see science in action inside a sandwich bag. Through this activity, children begin to understand that the process of decomposition is the natural decay of organisms and a continuing process in nature.

Materials

4 plastic zip closure sandwich bags

banana

knife

2 packets of yeast

water

Procedure

Label each one of the sandwich bags: "A," "B," "C," and "D." Prepare the bags as follows:

- Bag "A": put in several slices of banana
- Bag "B": put in several slices of banana and a packet of yeast
- Bag "C": put in several slices of banana and some water
- Bag "D": put in several slices of banana, some water, and a packet of yeast

Seal all the bags and place them on a sunny windowsill for a few days.

Results

The banana slices in bag "A" darken slightly. The yeast in bag "B" grows very slowly, but there is some change in the banana slices. The slices in bag "C" show some decay and some mold. The banana slices in bag "D" show the most decay. In that bag, the banana is breaking down. The liquid is bubbling, and carbon dioxide is forming and expanding the bag. The bag may pop open and release a powerful odor into the room.

Explanation

When plants and animals die, they serve as a valuable food source for microorganisms. These microorganisms feed on the dead materials and break them down. Yeast is made up of millions of such microorganisms, which grow under the right conditions: when moisture, food, and warmth are present. As they grow, the microorganisms in bag "D" break down the banana slices.

The same process takes place in nature. As a result, microorganisms can reduce large animals and plants into valuable nutrients for the soil. In other words, when an organism dies it provides what other organisms need to live.

SUGGESTED LITERATURE

Fredericks, Anthony D. *On One Flower: Butterflies, Ticks, and a Few More Icks.* Nevada City, CA: Dawn Publications, 2006.

Kalman, Bobbie, and Kathryn Smithyman. *The Life Cycle of a Frog.* New York: Crabtree Publishing, 2006.

Macnair, Patricia. *Life Cycle.* Boston: Houghton Mifflin, 2004.

Neye, Emily. *Butterflies.* New York: Grosset & Dunlap, 2000.

Riley, Peter D. *Life Cycles.* Milwaukee, WI: Gareth Stevens, 2003.

Weber, Rebecca. *The Cycle of Your Life.* Mankato, MN: Capstone Press, 2004.

Round and Round

(Life Cycles)

STAGING: All of the participants should be seated on stools. The narrator should be placed to the side of the other characters. She or he has a brief role at the beginning of the script and at the end.

	Miss Scientist X	Mrs. Mother X	Mr. Nurse X
Narrator X			
	Mr. Father X	Mr. Plumber X	Mrs. Banker X

NARRATOR: Welcome. We take you now to a discussion in our city. Several people are talking. They are asking questions. They are looking for answers. Let's listen in.

MR. FATHER: I heard something interesting [points to Miss Scientist]. I hope that you can help me.

MISS SCIENTIST: I'd be happy to. What is your question?

MR. FATHER: Well, I heard something on the radio. Some people were talking about life cycles. I thought that a cycle was what you rode on the street.

MISS SCIENTIST: No, that's a different kind of cycle. What they were talking about was the cycles of nature.

MRS. MOTHER: The cycles of nature. Is that how plants and animals live?

MISS SCIENTIST: Yes, that's part of it. But it's also something more.

MR. PLUMBER: What do you mean it's something more?

MISS SCIENTIST: Well, let's start with plants.

MRS. BANKER: That's good. Because I really like plants. In fact, I have a garden full of plants.

MISS SCIENTIST: That's good. Many of plants grow from seeds.

MRS. BANKER: Yes, each spring I put seeds in the ground. They start to grow. After some time I can gather them and eat them.

MISS SCIENTIST: You're right. But what if you didn't pick the beans or the corn or the squash? What would happen?

MR. NURSE: I know. The plants would die. They would fall on the ground and turn brown.

MRS. MOTHER: The dead plants could be put into a compost pile. That's where they decompose or break down. The next year they could be used to help new plants grow.

MISS SCIENTIST: Yes, yes indeed. That's part of what we call the "Cycle of Life."

MR. NURSE: Oh, I see. Plants grow from seeds. Then, after they finish growing they die. Then after they die they become food for other plants.

MISS SCIENTIST: You're right! But, let's take a look at animal life cycles.

MR. PLUMBER: I think I can figure this out. O.K. let's take a mouse, for example.

MRS. MOTHER: I don't like mice. They're not very nice. They're dirty creatures.

MR. PLUMBER: Well, you don't have to touch one. We just have to talk about one.

MRS. MOTHER: Well, O.K.

MR. FATHER: O.K., let's see if we can do this together. First, a mouse is born. It grows up. It eats lots of food. It has its own babies . . . .

MISS SCIENTIST: You're on the right track. Keep going.

MR. NURSE: I can help here. Sometime the mouse will die. When it dies its body begins to decompose.

MRS. BANKER: I don't know the word "decompose."

MR. PLUMBER: It means a dead plant or animal is broken down.

MISS SCIENTIST: That's right. The things that were part of the mouse's body go into the ground. They can now help other things grow, like plants.

MRS. BANKER: Can they help other mice?

MISS SCIENTIST: Yes, they can. When new plants grow mice will eat them. So the dead mouse can help other living mice. It does that because its body helps plants grow. And the plants help other mice grow.

MR. NURSE: I bet I know what you're going to say next. You're going to say that that is a cycle of life.

MISS SCIENTIST: Yes, that is a cycle of life. Every plant and every animal goes through a cycle. They are born. They grow and develop. And then they die. After they die, they help other plants and animals in their cycles.

MRS. MOTHER: Wow, life sure is amazing!

NARRATOR: Well, there you have it. The cycles of life as told by a circle of people. I guess everything just keeps going round and round and round and round.

A Machine World

(Simple Machines)

DISCIPLINE

Physical science

SCIENCE CONTENT STANDARD

Science and technology

SUMMARY

Simple machines are sometimes difficult for youngsters to understand. Constant and continual exposure to the principles and practices of simple machines in everyday life will help students appreciate their role as invaluable tools.

PROPS

Props are not necessary for this script. However, you may wish to provide each of the actors with an example of a simple machine to hold in her or his hands during the performance. As each character speaks, she or he can hold up her or his representative tool.

PRESENTATION SUGGESTIONS

Place a large sign around each of the 6 "simple machines" so that the audience is clear about each person's role. You may wish to draw a picture or attach illustrations of a representative machine on each placard to help the audience identify each character.

EXPERIMENT/ACTIVITY

Here's an activity that you may wish to use as a short-term or long-term exploration of simple machines.

Materials

duplicable chart (see below)

markers

Procedure

Create a duplicable chart similar to the one below. Provide students (individually or in small groups) with copies of the chart and invite them to identify examples of simple machines they locate in their homes, neighborhood, communities, on vacation, or at school (a few examples have been provided). You may wish to challenge students to locate at least 10 examples for each of the 6 categories.

Another option would be to organize a scavenger hunt—with students searching out examples of simple machines in and around the school within a designated time period (30 minutes, for example). Be sure to plan time so that students can review their respective lists and share thoughts and ideas about the value and utility of simple machines in everyday life.

SIMPLE MACHINE	EXAMPLES
Lever	shovel
Pulley	clothesline
Wheel & axle	doorknob
Inclined plane	stairs
Screw	drill
Wedge	knife

Results

Results will vary.

Explanation

Students will discover an interesting variety of simple machines in use throughout daily life as well as throughout their homes and communities. The 6 simple machines listed above are also part of many complex machines that we use everyday.

SUGGESTED LITERATURE

Fowler, Allan. *Simple Machines*. New York: Scholastic, 2001.

Glover, David. *Pulleys and Gears*. Chicago: Heinemann, 2006.

Parker, Lewis. *Simple Machines*. Des Moines, IA: Perfection Learning, 2005.

Tiner, John Hudson. *Wheels and Axles*. Mankato, MN: Smart Apple Media, 2002.

Tocci, Salvatore. *Experiments with Simple Machines*. New York: Children's Press, 2003.

A Machine World

(Simple Machines)

STAGING: The 2 narrators can stand in front and to the side of the other characters. The 6 major characters should be on stools or can be standing.

The Lever X	The Pulley X	The Wheel & Axle X
The Inclined Plane X	The Screw X	The Wedge X

Narrator 1	Narrator 2
X	X

NARRATOR 1: Today, we are going to introduce you to some machines.

NARRATOR 2: These are really some special machines.

NARRATOR 1: [points] They may not look like machines, but they are.

NARRATOR 2: Maybe, we should tell them what a machine does.

NARRATOR 1: O.K. A machine is something that makes work easier for people.

NARRATOR 2: That seems pretty simple.

NARRATOR 1: Well, we are going to meet some simple machines.

NARRATOR 2: So let me get this straight. A machine makes our work easier?

NARRATOR 1: Right.

NARRATOR 2: But I thought that a machine was something that was big and had a lot of parts.

NARRATOR 1: Well, those are machines, too. But something doesn't have to be big and noisy to be a machine.

NARRATOR 2: But, I thought that a machine was something you had to plug into the wall. I thought that a machine was something that used electricity.

NARRATOR 1: Well, some machines use electricity. But other machines use running water. Some use wind. Others use energy from the sun to make them work.

NARRATOR 2: O.K., now I understand. But what about those simple machines?

NARRATOR 1: I'm glad you asked. I brought along some simple machines. [points to the other characters] I'd like to show them to you.

NARRATOR 2: O.K., sounds good.

NARRATOR 1: Would each of you [points again] tell us about yourself?

THE LEVER: I'm a lever. I help to lift things up. I can be a bar that is used to lift a rock.

NARRATOR 2: My father lifts large rocks in the garden with a bar.

THE LEVER: Then he is using me. But, here's something else. A wheelbarrow is also a lever.

NARRATOR 1: I didn't know that.

THE LEVER: It's true. People use wheelbarrows to lift large loads. They carry them to a new place. Wheelbarrows are levers.

NARRATOR 2: What about you?

THE PULLEY: I'm a pulley. I help move things, too. I have a rope and one or more wheels. A person can pull down on the rope and lift a load.

NARRATOR 1: I've seen you being used on big ships.

THE PULLEY: You're right. People use me to lift big loads off big ships. Then they can raise them into the air. They can move them onto the docks.

THE WHEEL & AXLE: Like my friend here, [points to the Pulley] I have a wheel.

NARRATOR 2: But, isn't your wheel different?

THE WHEEL & AXLE: Yes, it is. I have a bar or a rod that goes through the middle of my wheel. My wheel goes around that bar. The wheels on your car use me. Each wheel is on an axle. Each wheel can turn around on each axle.

NARRATOR 1: That's cool. And, what about you [points to the Inclined Plane]? Why are you special?

THE INCLINED PLANE: I'm a simple machine, too. I sometimes have another name. Some people call me a ramp.

NARRATOR 2: Well, what do you do?

THE INCLINED PLANE: People use me to move things to a new level. You could use me to move something from a low level to a high level. Cars use freeway ramps to get from a low street level to a high level.

NARRATOR 1: That's neat! And, what about you [points to the Screw]?

THE SCREW: I'm a simple machine, too. I'm a cousin to my friend the Inclined Plane.

NARRATOR 2: Why is that?

THE SCREW: Because I'm an inclined plane that has been wrapped around something else. Look at a screw and you will see threads going round and round. They are in a spiral pattern.

NARRATOR 1: I know what you're going to say.

THE SCREW: Yes, a screw is an example of an inclined plane.

NARRATOR 2: How about our last simple machine [points to the Wedge]?

THE WEDGE: I'm a cousin to my friend the Inclined Plane.

NARRATOR 1: It sounds like the Inclined Plane has lots of relatives.

THE WEDGE: That's correct. I'm actually two inclined planes put back to back.

NARRATOR 2: Didn't I see you somewhere before?

THE WEDGE: Yes, you did. A knife is an example of a wedge. You use a knife to cut into something. If you look closely at a knife it's really an upside down triangle. It's really two inclined planes put back to back. A knife is really a wedge.

NARRATOR 1: Well, there you have it. Here are [points to all six characters] the six simple machines.

NARRATOR 2: And, you can find these six simple machines in all the tools we use. They're everywhere!

NARRATOR 1: They're our friends. And, now, they can be your friends, too.

ALL: Hip, Hip, Hooray!

Hip, Hip, Hooray!

Hip, Hip, Hooray!

Hear, Hear

(Sound)

DISCIPLINE

Physical science

SCIENCE CONTENT STANDARD

Position and motion of objects

SUMMARY

This script focuses on a basic definition of sound. Students learn that sound is caused by the vibration of an object. The faster an object vibrates, the higher the sound that is produced. The slower the vibration, the lower the sound.

PROPS

This readers theatre production requires 2 props. The first is a small box (matchbox, cardboard box) around which a rubber band has been wrapped. The second prop is created by tying a length of string (about 2 to 3 feet long) around the handle of a fork. Another fork is also provided. These props are placed on the table in the middle of the staging area.

PRESENTATION SUGGESTIONS

For this presentation students should all be standing up. You may wish to provide the "alien" with a simple paper mask or merely a sign indicating that she or he is a creature from another planet.

EXPERIMENT/ACTIVITY

Here's an interesting activity that will help demonstrate how vibrating objects produce sound waves.

Materials

small tub or pot

water

two forks

2- to 3-inch length of string

Procedure

Fill the pot or tub to the brim with water. Tie the length of string to the handle of the fork. Hold the string so that the tines of the fork are just over the surface of the water. Tap the fork with the other fork, causing it to vibrate. Invite students to listen to the sound created. Repeat again and quickly lower the tips of the fork tines into the water.

Results

The water will vibrate. Ripples will emanate from the vibrating tines, sending small ripples out to the edges of the pot or tub.

Explanation

The ripples are like small waves. They simulate the same types of waves that emanate from any vibrating object. We can't see sound waves as they move away from a vibrating object. But we can see the waves that move away from an object that is placed in water. Sound moves through the air in the same way that waves move through water.

SUGGESTED LITERATURE

Ciovacco, Justine, Bill Doyle, and Ruth Greenstein. *Sound*. Milwaukee, WI: Gareth Stevens, 2002.

Dreier, David Louis. *Sound*. Chanhassen, MN: Child's World, 2004.

Trumbauer, Lisa. *All About Sound*. New York: Children's Press, 2004.

Hear, Hear

(Sound)

Oye, Oye (El sonido)

STAGING: There is no narrator for this script. All the characters are standing around a small table or desk that has several props on it. From time to time, a character will pick up a prop and use it. Ask students to stand behind the desk (and face the audience) when handling a prop.

Student 1 X		Student 2 X
	(desk)	
Student 3 X		Alien Creature X

ALIEN CREATURE: Hello. My name is Gorgon and I'm from the planet Zero. I have come to your planet to learn all about science. On my planet we do not go to school. We just sit around all day and play with our computers. How boring! So I wanted to come to your planet to learn new things. I'm hoping you can help me.

EL EXTRATERRESTRE: Hola. Me llamo Gorgon y soy del planeta que se llama Cero. He venido a su planeta para aprender todo sobre las ciencias. En mi planeta, no asistimos a la escuela. Sólo pasamos todo el día sentado y jugando con las computadoras. ¡Qué aburrido! Pues, quería venir a su planeta para aprender cosas nuevas. Espero que puedan ayudarme.

STUDENT 1: Sure, we'll be happy to help you. We go to school all the time. And we learn lots of neat stuff. We have a terrific teacher [points] who teaches us some really cool things.

ESTUDIANTE 1: Por supuesto, nos alegramos de ayudarte. Asistimos a la escuela todo el tiempo. Y aprendemos muchas cosas interesantes. Tenemos un maestro fantástico [señala] que nos enseña algunas cosas muy divertidas.

STUDENT 2: What can we do to help you?

ESTUDIANTE 2: ¿En qué podemos ayudarte?

GORGON: Well, I have heard about this thing you call "sound." What is sound? We don't have any sound on the planet Zero. I'd like to know what it is.

GORGON: Pues, he oído de esta cosa que se llama el sonido. ¿Qué es el sonido? No tenemos ningún sonido en nuestro planeta Cero. Quisiera saber lo que es.

STUDENT 3: Well, first of all, sound happens when something vibrates.

ESTUDIANTE 3: Pues, primero, el sonido ocurre cuando algo vibra.

GORGON: What do you mean "vibrates?"

GORGON: ¿Qué significa <vibra?>

STUDENT 1: "Vibrates" means when something moves back and forth very fast.

ESTUDIANTE 1: <Vibra> significa que algo se mueve de acá para allá muy rápidamente.

GORGON: I saw a TV show from your planet. There dancers moving back and forth very quickly, like this [wiggles or shakes her or his body back and forth]. Is that what you mean by "vibrates?"

GORGON: Vi un programa de TV de su planeta. Había bailadores que se movían de acá para allá muy rápidamente así [se contonea y sacude el cuerpo de acá por allá]. ¿Es lo que significa <vibra?>

STUDENT 2: It's something like that.

ESTUDIANTE 3: Es algo así.

STUDENT 3: But, really, "vibrates" means when something moves back and forth really, really fast. When it moves back and forth really, really quickly it makes a sound.

ESTUDIANTE 3: Pero, de veras, <vibra> significa que algo se mueve de acá para allá muy rápidamente. Cuando se mueve de acá para allá muy rápidamente, hace un sonido.

GORGON: I don't understand. Can you show me something that moves back and forth really, really quickly?

GORGON: No entiendo. Puedes mostrarme algo que se mueve de acá para allá muy rápidamente.

STUDENT 1: Sure, let me show you [picks up the box with a rubber band stretched around it; plucks the rubber band]. Can you hear that sound?

ESTUDIANTE 1: Claro, permíteme mostrarte [levanta la caja que tiene una goma estirada alrededor; Tira la goma]. ¿Puedes oír el sonido?

GORGON: Yes, yes I can.

GORGON: Sí, sí, yo puedo.

STUDENT 1: Look closely and you can see the rubber band moving back and forth very, very fast. It's vibrating. It's vibrating so fast that it makes a sound. The sound you hear are the vibrations moving through the air.

ESTUDIANTE 1: Mira de cerca y puedes ver que la goma está moviendo de acá por allá muy, muy rápidamente. Está vibrando tan rápidamente que hace un sonido. El sonido que oyes son las vibraciones moviendo por el aire.

GORGON: Wow, that's cool! Show me something else.

GORGON: ¡Vaya, qué guay! Muéstrame algo más.

STUDENT 2: O.K., here's something really neat [picks up the fork/string devise and holds the end of the string with the fork hanging down; taps the hanging fork with the other fork to create a sound]! Can you hear the sound?

ESTUDIANTE 2: Bueno, aquí está algo muy interesante [levanta el aparato de cuchara y cuerda y toma el fin de la cuerda con la cuchara colgando; golpea suavemente la cuchara suspendida en el aire con la otra cuchara para crear un sonido]! ¿Puedes oír el sonido?

GORGON: Yes, yes I can.

GORGON: Sí, sí yo puedo.

STUDENT 1: When I tap the fork with another fork it makes the first fork vibrate. The first fork moves back and forth very fast. When it does it makes a sound. That's the sound you heard.

ESTUDIANTE 1: Cuando golpeo suavemente la cuchara con otra cuchara, hace una vibrar de la primera cuchara. La primera cuchara se mueve de acá para allá muy rápidamente. Cuando hace esto, crea un sonido. Eso es el sonido que oíste.

GORGON: Wow, you Earth kids are really smart. You must have a really smart teacher, too.

GORGON: Vaya, ustedes niños de la Tierra son tan listos. Su maestro debe que ser muy inteligente, también.

STUDENT 3: You're right about that!

ESTUDIANTE 3: ¡En eso tienes razón!

STUDENT 1: Here's something else you must know. When something vibrates it makes the air around it vibrate, too. Then the sound moves through the air. It goes into your ears. Inside your ears is something called an eardrum.

ESTUDIANTE 1: Aquí está algo más que debes saber. Cuando algo vibra, hace que el aire alrededor vibre también. El sonido se mueve por el aire. Entra tus oídos. Adentro de tus oídos, hay algo que se llama tu tímpano.

GORGON: Is it something like the drum in a band?

GORGON: ¿Es algo similar de un tambor de un grupo musical?

STUDENT 2: Yes, it's exactly like a drum. And, just like a drum it vibrates, too. That's when you actually hear the sound.

ESTUDIANTE 2: Sí, es exactamente como un tambor. Y como un tambor, su tímpano vibra también. Es entonces cuando oyes el sonido.

GORGON: Well you guys certainly taught me a lot. Thanks for telling me all about sound.

GORGON: Pues, amigos, por cierto me enseñaron mucho. Muchas gracias por decirme todo sobre el sonido.

STUDENT 3: You're welcome. Come back again sometime and we'll teach you some other cool stuff

ESTUDIANTE 3: De nada. Vuelve aquí otra vez y te enseñamos sobre otras cosas interesantes.

Let's Rock and Roll!

(Changes in the Earth)

DISCIPLINE

Earth science

SCIENCE CONTENT STANDARD

Changes in earth and sky

SUMMARY

The planet Earth is always in transition; it's always changing. Helping youngsters understand the dynamic nature of the planet we live on is an important science concept. Two of the most important terms involved with that concept are "weathering" and "erosion." This script introduces students to these vocabulary words.

PROPS

No props are needed for this script.

PRESENTATION SUGGESTIONS

You may wish to obtain some lab coats from your local high school for the characters to wear. Although much of the conversation takes place between the 2 characters, be sure to remind them to speak to the audience as well.

EXPERIMENT/ACTIVITY

I have used the following activity very successfully for many years. It's a great way to introduce students to the concept of erosion. Students make their own rocks and then rapidly wear them down.

Materials

clean sand

white glue (Elmer's®)

small container

plastic spoon

vegetable oil

aluminum foil

coffee can (with lid)

water

Procedure

Mix 3 large spoonfuls of sand together with 3 spoonfuls of white glue. Mix thoroughly (the mixture should be the consistency of heavy concrete). Make small lumps of the mixture and place them on a lightly oiled sheet of aluminum foil (the oil prevents the lumps from sticking to the foil).

Place the "rocks" in a dry, sunny location for 2 to 3 days, until hard. An alternative method is to place the aluminum sheet (with the sandy lumps) on a cookie sheet. Place the cookie sheet in an oven and heat to 250 degrees F. "Bake" the rocks for several hours.

When the "rocks" are thoroughly dry, put 3 or 4 of them into a coffee can with some water. Hold the lid on securely and shake the can for 4 to 5 minutes. Remove the lid.

Results

The "rocks" begin to wear down. Some of the "rocks" may be worn down into sand again.

Explanation

The water running over the "rocks" pushes them against each other, causing erosion that wears them down. In nature, this process takes many years, but the result is the same. Rocks are broken up, become smaller from rubbing against each other, and, over time, wear down into sandy particles that may eventually become part of the soil near a river or stream.

SUGGESTED LITERATURE

Bailey, Jacqui. *Cracking Up: A Story About Erosion*. Mankato, MN: Capstone Press, 2006.

Estigarribia, Diana. *Learning About Rocks, Weathering, and Erosion with Graphic Organizers*. New York: PowerKids Press, 2005.

Olien, Rebecca. *Erosion*. Mankato, MN: Capstone Press, 2001.

Spilsbury, Louise, and Richard Spilsbury. *The Disappearing Mountain and Other Earth Mysteries: Erosion and Weathering*. Austin, TX: Raintree, 2005.

Let's Rock and Roll!

(Changes in the Earth)

STAGING: This is a 2-person script with no narrator. The characters can be standing or seated on stools throughout the entire performance.

Scientist 1	Scientist 2
X	X

SCIENTIST 1: You know, I was just thinking about the planet Earth.

SCIENTIST 2: Why were you thinking about Earth?

SCIENTIST 1: Well, I think Earth is a pretty amazing place to live.

SCIENTIST 2: You're right, there.

SCIENTIST 1: It's amazing for many reasons. There is something really cool about the earth.

SCIENTIST 2: What's that?

SCIENTIST 1: Earth is always changing. Something is always happening to the earth.

SCIENTIST 2: You're right. Some of the changes take a long time. Some changes don't take much time at all.

SCIENTIST 1: The slow changes are the most interesting. Those are changes that take a long, l-l-l-o-o-o-n-n-n-g-g-g time. Like when the Grand Canyon was made.

SCIENTIST 2: What did you have in mind?

SCIENTIST 1: Well, "weathering," for one.

SCIENTIST 2: Yeah, I know what "weathering" is. Weathering is when rock is broken down at the earth's surface.

From *Nonfiction Readers Theatre for Beginning Readers* by Anthony D. Fredericks. Westport, CT: Teacher Ideas Press.
Copyright © 2007 by Anthony D. Fredericks.

SCIENTIST 1: That happens all the time. Water flows into the cracks of a large rock. Sometimes the water freezes. When water freezes, it expands. So when water in the crack of a rock freezes it, too, expands. Then the rock breaks apart.

SCIENTIST 2: That how big rocks are broken down into small rocks and pebbles. And, you know what? That happens all the time. Big rocks are being broken apart.

SCIENTIST 1: Yes, I know. But weathering happens when chemicals get onto rocks.

SCIENTIST 2: Chemicals. Oh, yes, now I remember. Sometimes there are chemicals in the air. There may be chemicals in water. When those chemicals get onto rocks they can break down the rocks.

SCIENTIST 1: Right, chemicals can cause weathering. It's something that is natural. It's something that happens all the time.

SCIENTIST 2: Weathering is one way that the earth is being changed. I believe there's another way. It's called erosion.

SCIENTIST 1: That's correct. Erosion is another way the earth is being changed. It, too, happens all the time.

SCIENTIST 2: Erosion is when the earth is worn down by water, ice or wind.

SCIENTIST 1: Yes. Glaciers move over the land and wear it down. That's erosion. Water in rivers and streams flows over rocks and wears them down. Dust and dirt in the wind blows over rocks and wears them down. All of those are forms of erosion.

SCIENTIST 2: Right. But we must remember something. Erosion takes a long, long time. It doesn't happen in just a few days. Or a few weeks. Or even a few years. It takes a long, l-l-l-o-o-o-n-n-n-g-g-g time.

SCIENTIST 1: So, I think we can agree. The earth is always changing.

SCIENTIST 2: Yes, it changes because of weathering.

SCIENTIST 1: And, it changes because of erosion.

SCIENTIST 2: Weathering and erosion. Two forces that are always changing the earth. Our world is always changing.

SCIENTIST 1: Wow, that's cool!

Far, Far Away

(Sun, Moon, and Planets)

DISCIPLINE

Space science

SCIENCE CONTENT STANDARD

Objects in the sky

SUMMARY

This script is a very brief introduction to the sun, moon, and 4 inner planets. Students will be stimulated to learn more about these celestial bodies in additional lessons and resources.

PROPS

No props are necessary for this production other than hand-lettered signs looped around each player's neck.

PRESENTATION SUGGESTIONS

Students should be standing throughout the production. In the beginning they remain in one place. Toward the end several of the characters begin moving (revolving) around the "sun."

EXPERIMENT/ACTIVITY

Here's an interesting activity/demonstration that will help students appreciate the enormous size of the sun.

Materials

30-foot length of string

measuring tape

quarter

Procedure

Go out onto the playground or field with your students. Form the string on the ground in the shape of a circle (invite students to assist you). The circle of string should be 9 feet in diameter. This circle represents the sun.

Place the quarter on the ground along one edge of the string circle. The quarter represents the earth.

Results

The equatorial diameter of the sun is 864,988 miles. The equatorial diameter of Earth is approximately 8,000 miles. That means that the diameter of the sun is about 108 times greater than the diameter of Earth.

Explanation

The string represents the sun, and the quarter (which is about 1 inch in diameter) represents earth. As you and your students look at the model you have created, you can begin to understand how much bigger the sun is than our own planet as well as every other planet in the solar system.

SUGGESTED LITERATURE

Birch, Robin. *Planets*. Broomall, PA: Chelsea Clubhouse, 2003.

Birch, Robin. *The Solar System*. Broomall, PA: Chelsea Clubhouse, 2003.

Gallant, Roy A. *The Planets*. Tarrytown, NY: Benchmark Books, 2001.

Lippincott, Kristen. *Astronomy*. New York: Dorling Kindersley, 2000.

Vogt, Gregory L. *Sun*. Mankato, MN: Capstone Press, 2000.

Far, Far Away

(Sun, Moon, and Planets)

Lejos, muy lejos (El sol, la luna, y los planetas)

STAGING: The narrator stands in front and to the side of the staging area. Most of the dialogue belongs to the narrator (the other characters have minor speaking roles). Each character should have a hand-lettered sign around her or his neck indicating what celestial body she or he is. The narrator remains stationary; the other characters will move around (as directed in the script).

```
                                              Moon
                                               X
                            Sun
                             X
             Earth
               X                      Mercury
                                         X
                                                        Venus
                                                          X
   Mars
    X

  Narrator
    X
```

NARRATOR: Welcome to the universe. My friends [points] and I will tell you a little about ourselves. First, I'd like you to meet the sun.

EL NARRADOR(A): Bienvenidos a nuestro universo. Mis amigos [señalando] y yo vamos a habarles un poco sobre nosotros mismos. Primero, quisiera presentarles el sol.

SUN: Hi [waves].

EL SOL: Hola [Saluda con la mano].

NARRATOR: The sun is shaped like a giant beach ball. Just like a beach ball, the sun is not solid. It is filled with lots of very hot gases. These gases give off lots of heat. All the heat on earth is produced by the sun. The surface temperature of the sun is over 11,000 degrees.

The sun is also a star. It is the most important star we know. It is the source of all life on Earth. Green plants need sunlight to grow. Animals eat plants for food. And, humans need plants and animals to live.

EL NARRADOR(A): El sol tiene la forma de una pelota de playa. Como la pelota de playa, el sol no es sólido. Está lleno de gases muy calientes. Estos gases producen mucho calor. El sol produce todo el calor del mundo. La temperatura de la superficie del sol es más de 11.000 grados.

El sol también es una estrella. Es la estrella más importante que conocemos. Es la fuente de toda la vida en la Tierra. Las plantas verdes necesitan la luz del sol para crecer. Los animales comen las plantas para comida. Y, los seres humanos necesitan las plantas y los animales para vivir.

SUN: That's right! I'm important to all you guys [points].

EL SOL: Correcto. Soy importante a todos Ustedes [señalando].

NARRATOR: The weather we have is made by the sun. The sun affects the temperature of the air. It also affects the amount of rainfall we have. It affects the clouds overhead. Everything on Earth needs the sun.

EL NARRADOR(A): El tiempo que tenemos es hecho por el sol. El sol afecta la temperatura del aire. También, afecta la cantidad de lluvia que tenemos. Afecta a las nubes por lo alto. Todo lo que está en la Tierra necesita el sol.

MOON: Hey, what about me [moves to the front of the staging area]?

LA LUNA: Oye, no se olviden de mí [se mueve al frente de la escena]?

NARRATOR: Now, here's our friend, the moon. The moon is the closest body in space to our planet. Humans have always been interested in the moon. Here's something interesting. The moon doesn't make its own light. The light we see is actually reflected sunlight.

EL NARRADOR(A): Ahora, aquí está nuestra amiga, la luna. La luna es el cuerpo espacial más cerca de nuestro planeta Los seres humanos siempre se han interesado en la luna. Aquí está algo interesante. La luna no hace su propia luz. La luz que vemos es realmente la luz reflejada del sol.

MOON: I'm really very bright. Get it? I'm really very BRIGHT!

LA LUNA: Soy de veras muy brillante. ¿Entienden? Soy de veras muy brillante.

NARRATOR: Anyway, the moon orbits or goes around the Earth. As it does its position in the sky changes. The direction of the sun's light on it also changes. This means that part of the moon has light and part of the moon is dark. These are known as the phases of the moon. The phases are different throughout the month.

EL NARRADOR(A): En fin, la luna gira alrededor de o viaja alrededor de la Tierra. Mientras hace esto, su posición en el cielo cambia. La dirección de la luz del sol en la luna también cambia. Esto significa que una parte de la luna tiene luz y la otra parte está oscura. Estas se llaman las fases de la luna. Las fases son diferentes por todo el mes.

MERCURY, VENUS, EARTH, MARS: [together] Hey, what about us?

MERCURIO, VENUS TIERRA, MARTE: [juntos] Oye, no se olviden de nosotros.

NARRATOR: Besides the sun and the moon, there are planets, too. Some of the planets include Mercury, the closest planet to the sun. Venus is the next planet. Next, comes our own planet, Earth. Then, comes Mars. There are several other planets besides these. They aren't here today. I think they're all out spinning around somewhere else.

Anyway, all these planets are going around the sun [the "planets" begin to walk around the "sun" in a clockwise rotation]. Each planet is different and each one is special.

EL NARRADOR(A): Además del sol y la luna, hay planetas, también. Algunos de los plantes incluyen Mercurio, el planeta más cerca del sol. Venus es el próximo planeta. Entonces, viene nuestro planeta, Tierra. Luego, viene Marte. Hay algunos planetas más aparte de estos. No están aquí hoy. Creo que están por allí girando en otro lugar.

En fin, todos los planetas giran alrededor del sol [los <planetas> empiezan a andar alrededor del <sol> en una rotación en el sentido de las agujas del reloj]. Cada planeta es distinto y especial.

MERCURY: It takes me only 88 days to go around the sun. The earth takes 365 days.

MERCURIO: Yo tardo sólo 88 días en girar alrededor del sol. La Tierra tarda 365 días.

VENUS: I'm the second planet. I was named for the Roman goddess of love.

VENUS: Soy el segundo planeta. Me nombraron por la diosa romana del amor.

EARTH: I'm really old—more than four and a half billion years old. Maybe I need a rocking chair, I'm so old.

TIERRA: Estoy muy vieja. Tengo más de cuatro mil millones y medio. Quizás necesite una mecedora, estoy tan vieja.

MARS: I have the largest volcano in the whole solar system. It's more than 17 miles high!

MARTE: Yo tengo el volcán más grande en todo el sistema solar. Es más de 17 millas de alta.

NARRATOR: Well, as you can see, there are lots of interesting things in the solar system. I hope you have a chance to learn more about all my friends here. It's a lot of fun!

EL NARRADOR(A): Pues, como pueden ver, hay muchas cosas interesantes en el sistema solar. Espero que tengan la oportunidad de aprender más sobre todos mis amigos aquí. ¡Es muy divertido!

All Together Now

(Communities)

DISCIPLINE

Communities

SOCIAL STUDIES CONTENT STANDARD

Civic ideals and practices

SUMMARY

This script provides students with a basic introduction to communities—what they are and how they function.

PROPS

The only prop necessary for this presentation is a fake microphone. You can construct one from construction paper rolled into a tube or shape a section of Styrofoam™ into a microphone.

PRESENTATION SUGGESTIONS

Invite students to stand throughout the presentation. The narrator can move around from person to person (with the fake microphone). After the presentation you may wish to discuss with students the specific elements of their local community that were mentioned in the script (stores, services, etc.).

EXPERIMENT/ACTIVITY

Here's a simple activity you may wish to share with your students.

Materials

None

Procedure

Divide students into several small groups. Invite each of the groups to conduct a survey of individuals in their local community. Students may wish to ask friends, neighbors, relatives, or other individuals about the various services or features of the local community. Ask students to assemble lists of the various types of community services they discover over a period of several days. Depending on the local community, students may wish to organize their collected information into a large chart such as the following (Note: This is only one suggestion. The dynamics of your local community may require other categories of information.)

Protection	Health	Stores	Recreation	Transportation
police	doctors	hardware	theater	buses
	nurses	clothing	park	traffic lights
		auto repair	playground	
		jeweler		

Results

Results will vary.

Explanation

If students live in a large community, you may wish to take time to discuss how the services in a smaller community might be different. If students live in a small community, talk about how a larger community may be different. Help students reach the conclusion that no matter what size a community may be, there are certain services that exist in every community, regardless of size.

SUGGESTED LITERATURE

Garza, Carmen Lomas. *In My Family*. New York: Children's Press, 2000.

Kalman, Bobbie. *What Is a Community? From A–Z*. Minneapolis, MN: Sagebrush, 1999.

Trumbauer, Lisa. *Communities*. Mankato, MN: Capstone Press, 2000.

All Together Now

(Communities)

Todos juntos ahora (Las comunidades)

STAGING: Each of the individuals should be standing or seated in a permanent position. The narrator moves from person to person with a fake or imaginary microphone. You may wish to designate the narrator as a reporter for one of your local TV stations.

Person 1 X		Person 2 X
	Narrator X	
Person 3 X		Person 4 X

NARRATOR: We are standing on the street looking at all the people. There seems to be many different people in this town. I'm hoping some of them can help me. Excuse me, can you answer a question for me?

EL NARRADOR(A): Estamos en la calle mirando a todas las personas. Parece que hay muchas personas distintas en esta ciudad. Espero que algunas de ellos puedan ayudarme. Disculpe ¿Podría contestarme una pregunta?

PERSON 1: I'd be happy to.

LA PERSONA 1: ¡Claro que sí!

NARRATOR: Well, can you tell me what a community is?

EL NARRADOR(A): Pues, ¿podría decirme lo que es una comunidad?

PERSON 1: It's been a long time since I was in school, but here goes. A community is a place where people live, work, and play.

LA PERSONA 1: Hace mucho tiempo que asistí a la escuela, pero aquí va. Una comunidad es un lugar en que las personas viven, trabajan, y juegan.

PERSON 2: And, don't forget one of the most important things about a community.

LA PERSONA 2: Y, no te olvides de una de las cosas más importantes sobre una comunidad

NARRATOR: What's that?

EL NARRADOR(A): ¿Qué es eso?

PERSON 2: People who live in a community depend on one another in many ways.

LA PERSONA 2: Las personas que viven en una comunidad dependen uno del otro.

NARRATOR: What do you mean?

EL NARRADOR(A): ¿Qué quieres decir?

PERSON 3: Maybe I can help. You see I may need some lumber to build a house. I can go to a store that sells lumber. The person working in that store is helping me by providing me with something that I need. In this case, it's lumber.

LA PERSONA 3: Es posible que pueda ayudar. Como ves, quizás necesite madera para construir una casa. Puedo ir a una tienda que vende la madera. La persona que trabaja en la tiene me ayuda vendiéndome algo que necesito. En este caso, es la madera.

PERSON 4: You're right. Let's say that I need some chocolate chip ice cream. I mean, I really really need some chocolate chip ice cream. Since I don't have any at home, I can go to the grocery store. Somebody there will sell me some chocolate chip ice cream. Yum, yum, yum. That person is helping me. Or, I depend on that person to sell me something I want.

LA PERSONA 4: Tienes razón. Digamos que necesito helado con pedacitos de chocolate. Digo, tengo una gran necesidad del helado con pedacitos de chocolate. Como no tengo nada en mi casa, puede ir al supermercado. Alguien allí me venderá helado con pedacitos de chocolate, ¡Qué sabroso! Esa persona me ayuda. O, cuento con esa persona para venderme algo que quiero.

NARRATOR: So, a community is where people sell things?

EL NARRADOR(A): Entonces, una comunidad es donde se venden cosas.

PERSON 3: It's actually more than that. It's also where people provide services.

LA PERSONA 3: Realmente, es más que eso. También, es donde las personas prestan servicios.

NARRATOR: What do you mean by that?

EL NARRADOR(A): ¿Qué quieres decir?

From *Nonfiction Readers Theatre for Beginning Readers* by Anthony D. Fredericks. Westport, CT: Teacher Ideas Press. Copyright © 2007 by Anthony D. Fredericks.

PERSON 1: Well, let's say you had a washing machine that didn't work. You don't know how to fix washing machines. So, you call somebody to come to your house. That person then fixes the broken washing machine.

LA PERSONA 1: Pues, digamos que tenía una lavadora que no funcionarse. No sabes arreglar lavadoras. Entonces, llamas a alguien que puede venir a tu casa. Esa persona arregla la lavadora rota.

PERSON 2: Or, let's say that your car is really dirty. You can take it to a car wash. Somebody there will wash the car for you.

LA PERSONA 2: O, digamos que tu coche está muy sucio. Puedes llevarlo a un túnel de lavado de coches. Alguien allí te lo lavará.

NARRATOR: Oh, I get it. People in a community provide services for other people in the same community.

EL NARRADOR(A): Ah, ya entiendo. Las personas en las comunidades prestan servicios para otras personas en la misma comunidad.

PERSON 4: That's right! A community is made up of people who sell things. And, a community is made up of people who provide services.

LA PERSONA 4: ¡Correcto! Una comunidad consiste en las personas que venden productos. Y una comunidad consiste en las personas que prestan servicios.

NARRATOR: What are some of the other services in a community?

EL NARRADOR(A): ¿Cuáles son algunos de los otros servicios en una comunidad?

PERSON 3: A school is a service that every community has. A library is a service in many communities. Stores, gas stations, banks, hardware stores, hospitals, police and firefighters are all community services.

LA PERSONA 3: Una escuela es un servicio que cada comunidad tiene. Una biblioteca es un servicio en muchas comunidades. Las tiendas, las estaciones de gasolina, los bancos, las ferreterías, los hospitales, la policía, y los bomberos son servicios de las comunidades.

PERSON 1: There's one more thing that every community has.

LA PERSONA 1: Hay una cosa más que tiene cada comunidad.

NARRATOR: What's that?

EL NARRADOR(A): ¿Qué es eso?

PERSON 1: Most communities have people who make the rules. They have people who make the laws for the community.

LA PERSONA 1: La mayoría de las comunidades tienen personas que hacen reglas. Tienen personas que hacen las leyes para la comunidad.

PERSON 2: The rules of laws are important. They make sure everyone does the right thing. They make sure everyone is safe and protected.

LA PERSONA 2: Las reglas de las leyes son muy importantes. Aseguran que todas las personas hagan las cosas correctas. Aseguran que todos no estén en peligro y que estén protegidos.

PERSON 3: Yeah, there are rules for traffic in the community. There are rules about littering and pollution. There are rules for noise. There are rules for . . .

LA PERSONA 3: Si, hay reglas del tráfico en la comunidad. Hay reglas sobre la basura y la contaminación. Hay reglas para el ruido. Hay reglas para . . .

NARRATOR: . . . It seems like there are lots of rules in a community.

EL NARRADOR(A): . . . Parece que hay muchas reglas en una comunidad.

PERSON 4: It may seem that way. Actually, the rules are there so everyone is treated the same. Everyone is protected.

LA PERSONA 4: Tal vez parezca que sí. En verdad, hay reglas para que todos reciban el mismo trato. Todo el mundo es protegido.

PERSON 1: But, the best thing is that people are always around to help. If someone is sick, there are people to help. If a terrible storm damages property, there's someone to help. If someone is handicapped or needs a special service, there is always someone around to help.

LA PERSONA 1: Pero, lo mejor es que siempre hay personas para ayudar. Si alguien está enfermo, hay personas para ayudar. Si una tormenta terrible destruye algo, hay alguien para ayudar. Si alguien tiene problemas con moverse o necesita servicios especiales, siempre hay alguien que puede ayudar.

NARRATOR: O.K., now I get it. A community is people helping people.

EL NARRADOR(A): ¡Está bien! Entiendo ahora. Una comunidad es personas que se ayudan.

PERSON 1: Right. And, it's a place where people live . . .

LA PERSONA 1: Así es. Y, es un lugar donde las personas viven . . .

PERSON 2: . . . and work . . .

LA PERSONA 2: . . . y trabajan . . .

PERSON 3: . . . and play . . .

LA PERSONA 3: . . . y juegan . . .

PERSON 4: . . . and share.

LA PERSONA 4: . . . y comparten.

It's the Law!

(Needing Rules and Laws)

DISCIPLINE

Nation and country

SOCIAL STUDIES CONTENT STANDARD

Civic ideals and practices

SUMMARY

As citizens, we must all be aware of the rules and laws that help keep us safe and protect us from harm. Students, too, must have a basic understanding of the rules and processes that make their community a safe place to learn, play, and live in. This script can serve as an introduction to a unit on laws and rules.

PROPS

There are no props required for this script.

PRESENTATION SUGGESTIONS

It is suggested that students be seated on stools or chairs for this presentation. However, you may wish to have each character get off her or his stool and step to the front of the staging area just before delivering her or his lines (each character, save one, only has one speaking part). Additional characters can step forward to deliver their lines.

EXPERIMENT/ACTIVITY

The following activit(ies) should be made part of any discussion or textbook chapter on "rules and laws."

Materials

   None

Procedure

Students should be involved in examples of self-governance. Here are 2 possibilities:

1. Designate yourself as president of the class. Assemble a cabinet designating students (on a rotating basis) for specific roles. For example:

     - Secretary of Transportation—makes sure students get to the buses on time each day.

     - Secretary of Labor—designates students for various classroom jobs.

     - Secretary of the Treasury—counts the lunch money each day.

     - Secretary of State—shares classroom discoveries with students in other classes.

     - Attorney General—makes sure the rules of the classroom are adhered to by all.

2. Hold a "town" election. Elect a mayor for your class. Then, working with the new mayor, assemble various people and/or groups for your "town."

     - Judge—rules on all disputes or infractions of rules.

     - Police Officer—checks to be sure rules are followed.

     - Lawyer—serves as a "legal counsel" for any disputes.

     - Town Council—passes a series of rules.

Results

Depending on the format you select, the results can be long-lasting (retaining the designated positions throughout the school year) or short-term (just for the length of the unit).

Explanation

Students will get a sense of all the elements, components, and people that are necessary for the efficient running, governance, and maintenance of a municipality.

SUGGESTED LITERATURE

Miller, Jake. *Community Rules: Making and Changing Rules and Laws in Communities*. New York: PowerKids Press, 2005.

Sobel, Syl. *How the U.S. Government Works*. Hauppauge, NY: Barrons, 1999.

It's the Law!

(Needing Rules and Laws)

STAGING: There is no narrator for this script. The characters may all be standing or seated on stools.

Judge	Police Officer	Mayor	Government
X	X	X	X
Law	Town	City Council	Lawyer
X	X	X	X

TOWN: Hi, I'm a town. Now you may think that I look kind of funny to be a town. But, really I'm a town. I'm just like the town you live in. There are people who live here. There are people who work here. And, there are people who play here. Lots of people live and work and play in a town. I may be big or I may be small. But, I'm still a town. People in a town want to feel safe. People in a town want to know that they are protected. That's why they need my friend here [points to "Law"]. I'm going to let her tell you more.

LAW: Hi, I'm a law. You can find me in most towns or cities. People make me. They make me so that they are safe. A law is a rule that everybody must follow. Some laws are made to protect property. Some laws are made to protect people. It's important for everybody to follow me. If they don't they may be hurt. If they don't other people may be hurt. Laws are for everybody.

POLICE OFFICER: Hi, I'm a police officer. I am in your town, too. I am there to help everybody obey the laws. To obey means to follow. It means that everybody knows how to behave. My job to make sure that everybody is protected. Sometimes people don't want to follow the laws. Sometimes they don't want to obey the laws. They want to do what they want to do. That may mean that somebody gets hurt. That may mean that property is hurt. My job is to protect all the people and all the property. Sometimes people don't follow the laws. Then, part of my job is to find that person and arrest them. Sometimes I don't like to do that. But, that's my job.

LAWYER: Hi, I'm a lawyer. A lawyer is someone who knows about the law. I went to college to learn a lot about laws. I had to take a special test to make sure I knew about laws. My job is to help people when laws are broken. Sometimes I will help a person who has been told that they broke the law. I see if they really did break the law. I try to protect them. Or, maybe there is a bad person who really wants to break the law. Then, I will work to put that person in jail. I will work with the police officer to make sure that happens. Or, I will work with a judge.

JUDGE: Hi, I'm a judge. I work with the police officer and the lawyer. My job is like theirs. I work to make sure that people are protected. And, I work to make sure that property is protected. If a law is broken, people come to see me. I work in a courthouse. Your town has a courthouse. It's where lawyers and judges both work. If somebody believes that a law has been broken they come to the courthouse. There, I will listen to their story. I will listen to the stories of other people. Then, I will make a decision. I will say if the person broke the law. I may also say that the person did not break the law. My job is tough. Sometimes I must make some hard choices. But, I'm always thinking about the law. I'm always thinking about protecting people. I'm always thinking about protecting property.

CITY COUNCIL: Hi. I'm the city council. Actually I'm a group of people in your town. We are usually elected by the people in the town. They elect us to make laws. They elect us to protect them. They elect us to protect their property. We meet as a group. We talk about lots of things. We talk about how to make our town a good place to live. We talk about how to make our schools better. We talk about how businesses can help people. We talk about where we can get money. It's not an easy job. But it's a job that is important so everyone can be happy and safe.

MAYOR: I'm the mayor. You can find me in most towns. I'm like the president of the town. I was in an election. The people of the town elected me. They thought that I would be the best person to run the town. I work with all my friends here [points]. We are all working to make sure our town is safe and protected. I help to get money to make all that happen. I work to make sure there are enough firefighters in our town. I work to make sure there are enough police officers in our town. I make sure that poor people or sick people are taken care of in our town. I also tell other people that our town is the best place to live. That's because we all are protected in this town. It's a safe place to live.

GOVERNMENT: I am all the laws and rules in the town. I am all the people in the town. They make sure that all the laws and rules are followed. I'm actually a group of people who make the rules and laws and see that they are obeyed. I help keep order. I help to settle arguments. And, I help keep people and their property safe from harm. I am everything you have heard all wrapped up in one. I am government. I may be the most important thing of all.

TOWN: So, there you have it. I'm just like where you live. And, my friends here [points] are just like the friends where you live, too. Get to know them. They are there to protect you and make you safe. Just like me, your town is a very special place because of all these friends here.

Resources

READERS THEATRE BOOKS

Barchers, S. *Fifty Fabulous Fables: Beginning Readers Theatre*. Westport, CT: Teacher Ideas Press, 1997.

———. *Judge for Yourself*. Westport, CT: Teacher Ideas Press, 2004.

———. *Muticultural Folktales: Readers Theatre for Elementary Students*. Westport, CT: Teacher Ideas Press, 2000.

———. *Readers Theatre for Beginning Readers*. Westport, CT: Teacher Ideas Press, 1993.

———. *Scary Readers Theatre*. Westport, CT: Teachers Ideas Press, 1994.

Barchers, S., and C. R. Pfeffinger. *More Readers Theatre for Beginning Readers*. Westport, CT: Teacher Ideas Press, 2006.

Barnes, J. W. *Sea Songs*. Westport, CT: Teacher Ideas Press, 2004.

Black, A. N. *Born Storytellers*. Westport, CT: Teacher Ideas Press, 2005.

Criscoe, B. L., and P. J. Lanasa. *Fairy Tales for Two Readers*. Westport, CT: Teacher Ideas Press, 1995.

Dixon, N., A. Davies, and C. Politano. *Learning with Readers Theatre: Building Connections*. Winnipeg, Manitoba: Peguis Publishers, 1996.

Fredericks, A. D. *Frantic Frogs and Other Frankly Fractured Folktales for Readers Theatre*. Westport, CT: Teacher Ideas Press, 1993.

———. *Mother Goose Readers Theatre for Beginning Readers*. Westport, CT: Teacher Ideas Press, 2007.

———. *Readers Theatre for American History*. Westport, CT: Teacher Ideas Press, 2001.

———. *Science Fiction Readers Theatre*. Westport, CT: Teacher Ideas Press, 2002.

———. *Silly Salamanders and Other Slightly Stupid Stories for Readers Theatre*. Westport, CT: Teacher Ideas Press, 2000.

———. *Tadpole Tales and Other Totally Terrific Treats for Readers Theatre*. Westport, CT: Teacher Ideas Press, 1997.

Garner, J. *Wings of Fancy: Using Readers Theatre to Study Fantasy Genre*. Westport, CT: Teacher Ideas Press, 2006

Georges, C., and C. Cornett. *Reader's Theatre*. Buffalo, NY: D.O.K. Publishers, 1990.

Haven, K. *Great Moments in Science: Experiments and Readers Theatre*. Westport, CT: Teacher Ideas Press, 1996.

Jenkins, D. R. *Just Deal with It*. Westport, CT: Teacher Ideas Press, 2004.

Johnson, T. D., and D. R. Louis. *Bringing It All Together: A Program for Literacy*. Portsmouth, NH: Heinemann, 1990.

Latrobe, K. H., C. Casey, and L. A. Gann. *Social Studies Readers Theatre for Young Adults.* Westport, CT: Teacher Ideas Press, 1991.

Laughlin, M. K., P. T. Black, and K. H. Latrobe. *Social Studies Readers Theatre for Children.* Westport, CT: Teacher Ideas Press, 1991.

Laughlin, M. K., and K. H. Latrobe. *Readers Theatre for Children.* Westport, CT: Teacher Ideas Press, 1990.

Martin, J. M. *12 Fabulously Funny Fairy Tale Plays.* New York: Instructor Books, 2002.

Peterson, C. *Around the World Through Holidays.* Westport, CT: Teacher Ideas Press, 2005.

Pfeffinger, C. R. *Character Counts.* Westport, CT: Teacher Ideas Press, 2003.

———. *Holiday Readers Theatre.* Westport, CT: Teacher Ideas Press, 1994.

Pugliano-Martin, C. *25 Just-Right Plays for Emergent Readers (Grades K–1).* New York: Scholastic, 1999.

Shepard, A. *Folktales on Stage: Children's Plays for Readers Theatre.* Olympia, WA: Shepard Publications, 2003.

———. *Readers on Stage: Resources for Readers Theatre.* Olympia, WA: Shepard Publications, 2004.

———. *Stories on Stage: Children's Plays for Readers Theatre.* Olympia, WA: Shepard Publications, 2005.

Sloyer, S. *From the Page to the Stage.* Westport, CT: Teacher Ideas Press, 2003.

Wolf, J. M. *Cinderella Outgrows the Glass Slipper and Other Zany Fractured Fairy Tale Plays.* New York: Scholastic, 2002.

Wolfman, J. *How and Why Stories for Readers Theatre.* Westport, CT: Teacher Ideas Press, 2004.

Worthy, J. *Readers Theatre for Building Fluency: Strategies and Scripts for Making the Most of This Highly Effective, Motivating, and Research-Based Approach to Oral Reading.* New York: Scholastic, 2005.

WEB SITES

http://www.aaronshep.com/rt/RTE.html

How to use readers theatre, sample scripts from a children's author who specializes in readers theatre, and an extensive list of resources.

http://www.cdli.ca/CITE/langrt.htm

This site has lots of information, including What Is Readers Theatre, Readers Theatre Scripts, Writing Scripts, Recommended Print Resources, and Recommended Online Resources.

http://www.teachingheart.net/readerstheater.htm

Here you discover lots of plays and lots of scripts to print and read in your classroom or library.

http://literacyconnections.com/readerstheater

There is an incredible number of resources and scripts at this all-inclusive site.

http://www.proteacher.com/070173.shmtl

This site is a growing collection of tens of thousands of ideas shared by teachers across the United States and around the world.

http://www.readerstheatredigest.com

    This is an online magazine of ideas, scripts, and teaching strategies.

http://www.readerstheatre.escd.net

    This site has over 150 short poems, stories, and chants for readers theatre.

http://www.storycart.com

    Storycart's Press's subscription service provides an inexpensive opportunity to have timely scripts delivered to teachers or librarians each month. Each script is created or adapted by well-known writer Suzanne Barchers, author of several readers theatre books (see above).

PROFESSIONAL ORGANIZATION

Institute for Readers Theatre
P.O. Box 421262
San Diego, CA 92142
(858) 277-4274
http://www.readerstheatreinstitute.com

Teacher Resources

by

Anthony D. Fredericks

The following books are available from Teacher Ideas Press (88 Post Road West, Westport, CT 06881); 1-800-225-5800; http://www.teacherideaspress.com.

Frantic Frogs and Other Frankly Fractured Folktales for Readers Theatre. ISBN 1-56308-174-1 (123pp.; $19.50)

Have you heard "Don't Kiss Sleeping Beauty, She's Got Really Bad Breath" or "The Brussels Sprouts Man (The Gingerbread Man's Unbelievably Strange Cousin)"? This resource (grades 4–8) offers 30 reproducible, satirical scripts for rip-roaring dramatics in any classroom or library.

The Integrated Curriculum: Books for Reluctant Readers, Grades 2–5. 2nd ed. ISBN 0-87287-994-1. (220pp.; $22.50).

This book presents guidelines for motivating and using literature with reluctant readers. The book contains more than 40 book units on titles carefully selected to motivate the most reluctant readers.

Investigating Natural Disasters Through Children's Literature: An Integrated Approach. ISBN 1-56308-861-4. (193pp.; $28.00).

Tap into students' inherent awe of storms, volcanic eruptions, hurricanes, earthquakes, tornadoes, floods, avalanches, landslides, and tsunamis to open their minds to the wonders and power of the natural world.

Involving Parents Through Children's Literature: P–K. ISBN 1-56308-022-2. (86pp; $15.00).

Involving Parents Through Children's Literature: Grades 1–2. ISBN 1-56308-012-5. (95pp.; $14.50).

Involving Parents Through Children's Literature: Grades 3–4. ISBN 1-56308-013-3. (96pp.; $15.50).

Involving Parents Through Children's Literature: Grades 5–6. ISBN 1-56308-014-1. (107pp.; $16.00).

This series of 4 books offers engaging activities for adults and children that stimulate comprehension and promote reading enjoyment. Reproducible activity sheets based on high-quality children's books are designed in a convenient format so that children can take them home.

The Librarian's Complete Guide to Involving Parents Through Children's Literature: Grades K–6. ISBN 1-56308-538-0. (137pp.; $24.50).

Activities for 101 children's books are presented in a reproducible format, so librarians can distribute them to students to take home and share with parents.

More Social Studies Through Children's Literature: An Integrated Approach. ISBN 1-56308-761-8. (225pp.; $27.50).

Energize your social studies curriculum with dynamic, "hands-on, minds-on" projects based on such great children's books as *Amazing Grace*, *Fly Away Home*, and *Lon Po Po*. This book is filled with an array of activities and projects sure to "energize" any social studies curriculum.

Mother Goose Readers Theatre for Beginning Readers. ISBN 1-59158-500-7.

Designed especially for educators in the primary grades, this resource provides engaging opportunities that capitalize on children's enjoyment of Mother Goose rhymes. There is lots to share and lots to enjoy in the pages of this resource.

Readers Theatre for American History. ISBN 1-56308-860-6. (173pp.; $30.00).

This book offers a participatory approach to American history in which students become active participants in several historical events. These 24 scripts give students a "you are there" perspective on critical milestones and colorful moments that have shaped the American experience.

Science Adventures with Children's Literature: A Thematic Approach. ISBN 1-56308-417-1. (190pp.; $24.50).

Focusing on the National Science Education Standards, this activity-centered resource uses a wide variety of children's literature to integrate science across the elementary curriculum. With a thematic approach, it features the best in science trade books along with stimulating hands-on, minds-on activities in all the sciences.

Science Discoveries on the Net: An Integrated Approach. ISBN 1-56308-823-1. (315pp.; $27.50).

This book is designed to help teachers integrate the Internet into their science programs and enhance the scientific discoveries of students. The 88 units emphasize key concepts—based on national and state standards—throughout the science curriculum.

Silly Salamanders and Other Slightly Stupid Stuff for Readers Theatre. ISBN 1-56308-825-8. (161pp.; $23.50).

The third entry in the "wild and wacky" readers theatre trilogy is just as crazy and just as weird as the first two. This unbelievable resource offers students in grades 3–6 dozens of silly send-ups of well-known fairy tales, legends, and original stories.

Social Studies Discoveries on the Net: An Integrated Approach. ISBN 1-56308-824-X. (276pp.; $26.00).

This book is designed to help teachers integrate the Internet into their social studies programs and enhance the classroom discoveries of students. The 75 units emphasize key concepts—based on national and state standards—throughout the social studies curriculum.

Social Studies Through Children's Literature: An Integrated Approach. ISBN 1-87287-970-4. (192pp.; $24.00).

Each of the 32 instructional units contained in this resource utilizes an activity-centered approach to elementary social studies, featuring children's picture books such as *Ox-Cart Man, In Coal Country,* and *Jambo Means Hello.*

Tadpole Tales and Other Totally Terrific Titles for Readers Theatre. ISBN 1-56308-547-X. (115pp.; $18.50).

A follow-up volume to the best selling *Frantic Frogs and Other Frankly Fractured Folktales for Readers Theatre,* this book provides primary level readers (grades 1–4) with a humorous assortment of wacky tales based on well-known Mother Goose rhymes. More than 30 scripts and dozens of extensions will keep students rolling in the aisles.

Nonfiction Children's Books

by

Anthony D. Fredericks

Amazing Animals. Minnetonka, MN: NorthWord Press, 2000. [grades 3–6]

Animal Sharpshooters. New York: Watts, 1999. [grades 4–6]

Around One Cactus: Owls, Bats and Leaping Rats. Nevada City, CA: Dawn Publications, 2003. [grades 1–4]. 2004 Teacher's Choice Award (International Reading Association); 2004 Teacher's Choice Award (*Learning Magazine*).

Bloodsucking Creatures. New York: Watts, 2002. [grades 3–6]

Cannibal Animals: Animals That Eat Their Own Kind. New York: Watts, 1999. [grades 4–6]

Clever Camouflagers. Minnetonka, MN: NorthWord Press, 2000. [grades 3–6]

Elephants for Kids. Minnetonka, MN: NorthWord Press, 1999. [grades 2–4]

Exploring the Oceans: Science Activities for Kids. Golden, CO: Fulcrum Publishing, 1998. [grades 3–8]

Exploring the Rainforest: Science Activities for Kids. Golden, CO: Fulcrum Publishing, 1996. [grades 3–8]

Exploring the Universe: Science Activities for Kids. Golden, CO: Fulcrum Publishing, 2000. [grades 3–8]

Fearsome Fangs. New York: Watts, 2002. [grades 3–6]

In One Tidepool: Crabs, Snails and Salty Tails. Nevada City, CA: Dawn Publications, 2002. [grades 1–4]

Moose. Minnetonka, MN: NorthWord Press, 2000. [grades 2–4]

Near One Cattail: Turtles, Logs and Leaping Frogs. Nevada City, CA: Dawn Publications, 2005. [grades 1–4]. 2005 Green Earth Book Award (Newton Marasco Foundation); 2006 Nature and Ecology Honor Book (*Skipping Stones Magazine*).

No Sweat Science: Nature Experiments. New York: Sterling Publishing, 2005.

On One Flower: Butterflies, Ticks and a Few More Icks. Nevada City, CA: Dawn Publications, 2006. [grades 1–4]

Slugs. Minneapolis, MN: Lerner Publications, 1999. [grades 1–3]. 2000 Outstanding Science Trade Book (National Science Teachers Association/Children's Book Council).

Surprising Swimmers. Minnetonka, MN: NorthWord Press, 2000. [grades 3–6]

Tsunami Man: Learning About Killer Waves with Walter Dudley. Honolulu: University of Hawaii Press, 2002. [grades 4–8]

Under One Rock: Bugs, Slugs and Other Ughs. Nevada City, CA: Dawn Publications, 2001. [grades 1–4]. 2002 Ecology and Nature Award (*Skipping Stones Magazine*); 2003 Teacher's Choice Award (*Learning Magazine*).

Weird Walkers. Minnetonka, MN: NorthWord Press, 2000. [grades 3–6]

Wild Animals. Minnetonka, MN: NorthWord Press, 2000. [grades 3–6]

Zebras. Minneapolis, MN: Lerner Publications, 2000. [grades 1–3]

. . . AND ONE FICTION BOOK

The Tsunami Quilt: Grandfather's Story. Chelsea, MI: Sleeping Bear Press, 2007. [grades 2–5]

Index

About the Author

Anthony (Tony) D. Fredericks (afredericks60@comcast.net) is a nationally recognized children's literature expert well known for his energetic, humorous, and highly informative school visits throughout North America. His dynamic author presentations have captivated thousands of students in Canada, Mexico, and across the United States—all with rave reviews!

Tony is a former elementary teacher and reading specialist. He is the author of more than 100 books, including over 65 teacher resource books and more than three dozen award-winning children's books. His education titles include the best-selling *Science Fair Handbook* (3d ed.), which he co-authored with Isaac Asimov (Goodyear), the hugely popular *Frantic Frogs and Other Frankly Fractured Folktales for Readers Theatre* (Teacher Ideas Press), the highly praised *Guided Reading in Grades 3–6* (Harcourt Achieve), and the celebrated *Much More Social Studies Through Children's Literature* (Teacher Ideas Press).

His award-winning children's titles include *Under One Rock* (2002 Nature and Ecology Award); *Slugs* (2000 Outstanding Science Trade Book), *Around One Cactus* (2004 Teacher's Choice Award), *Near One Cattail* (2006 Green Earth Book Award), and *The Tsunami Quilt: Grandfather's Story,* among others.

Fredericks is the author of several trade books including the perennial favorite *The Complete Idiot's Guide to Success as a Teacher* (Alpha) and the acclaimed *The Complete Idiot's Guide to Teaching College* (Alpha). Tony currently teaches elementary methods courses and children's literature at York College in York, Pennsylvania.